A Theory For All Music

Book One: Fundamentals

Kenneth P. Langer

Brass Bell Books

Brass Bell
Books & Games

Copyright © 2018 K. Langer

First Edition, 2018
Version 1.2, 2024: Revised

All rights reserved

No part of this book may be reproduced, or stored in a retrieval system, or transmitted in any form or by any means, electronic, mechanical, photocopying, recording, or otherwise, without express written permission of the publisher.

Published by Brass Bell Books and Games
www.brassbellbooks.com

Printed in the United States of America

Contents

Title Page	
Copyright	
Introduction	1
Unit One	6
Lesson 111	7
Lesson 112	11
Lesson 113	18
Lesson 114	21
Lesson 115	25
Unit Two	32
Lesson 121	33
Lesson 122	39
Lesson 123	45
Lesson 124	53
Lesson 125	58
Unit Three	64
Lesson 131	65
Lesson 132	75
Lesson 133	80
Lesson 134	86

Unit Four	96
Lesson 141	97
Lesson 142	103
Lesson 143	109
Unit Five	114
Lesson 151	115
Lesson 152	120
Lesson 153	125
Lesson 154	132
Lesson 155	138
Exercise Answers	142
Unit One Answers	143
Unit Two Answers	148
Unit Three Answers	153
Unit Four Answers	159
Unit Five Answers	162
Other Books	171
Final Note	173

Introduction

The purpose of this project is to provide materials for a two year college music theory course. Its goal is to describe and administer the tools of Western music analysis through the parameters or basic elements of music but in a way that allows those tools to be used to understand the music of any culture, style, or historical period.

This theory sequence will focus primarily on Western musical notation and analysis since that is the culture from which I and most of my students are immersed but it is also focused on finding a way to analyze all kinds of music regardless of style, culture, or period. To do this we must look at more than just harmony upon which most theory textbooks center. Music of the Western Classical tradition tends to be driven by harmony but not all styles of music are so oriented. However, all music does use the same five elements or parameters of music in different ways. The five parameters are melody, rhythm, harmony, texture, and form. By thoroughly understanding these parameters and all their constituent elements can we hope to understand different kinds of music.

The Parameters of Music

- Melody
- Rhythm
- Harmony
- Texture (and Timbre)
- Form

The first parameter, melody, is by far the easiest to hear. It is also the parameter which is usually emphasized the most. A melody is a set of pitches conceived in a horizontal fashion and which develops its own unique character. Rhythm deals with the duration of pitches and silence in relation to time. Harmony deals with stacked pitches that support the melody. Texture deals with the relationship between melody and harmony and with other inner workings of the music. Timbre is how we describe the unique sound of an instrument or a group of instruments. (In this text, I am combining Timbre into the category of Texture.) Form is the overall structure of a work of music created through the repetition and contrast of musical ideas.

By using these parameters and several of the characteristics associated with each we can formulate a set of questions to help us analyze music from many different time periods, styles, and even cultural backgrounds. This is because all music use these same parameters but in different ways. Western Classic music may emphasize harmony and harmonic functions but other styles emphasize other things.

It is like comparing pizzas. Everyone knows what a pizza is but there are different styles of pizza. In order to understand the differences we have to know how a pizza is put together. There are three main elements to a pizza: the dough (crust), the sauce, and the toppings. If we analyze these separately we can determine how one pizza is different from another. For example, a Chicago style pizza has a thick crust while a traditional New York style pizza has a thin crust. Most pizzas use a red tomato sauce but Greek pizzas are often white because they use white cheese instead. If we only looked at pizza sauces we would not be able to understand the differences between New York and Chicago pizzas. If we only looked at crusts we could not appreciate the different tastes of red or white pizzas. We need to understand all the elements, notice which ones are being used, and make sense of how they are being used to create a particular sensation.

Why Analysis Is Important

Music Theory students constantly ask why they are required to study the subject of music theory and for good reason. The study of music theory can be difficult and arduous but it can also be very important to the musician–regardless of the specific musical pursuit.

Music theory used to be the main study for future composers. They studied the compositional techniques of the past. Patterns of use for these techniques were observed and then given specific names. It is not that composers like Bach sat at his organ and said to himself "this is a great place to put in a secondary dominant chord." Composers write music from the heart (and the mind) and from a desire to create an emotional experience through sound. Their particular choices of notes and combinations come from their own study of music and from a desire to create something new. It is the theorists who give names to patterns and structures and tell us how composers tended to use them. Music theory helps composers understand what composers of the past have done not to imitate them but to develop a ground of understanding from which to grow and develop new ideas. New plants cannot grow without being rooted in soil and soil is made up of the all the plants that have come before it.

Music performers can also benefit from the study of music theory. By understanding a piece of music thoroughly and by knowing the intentions of the composer (as much as that can be possible) the performer learns how to express that piece of music with a deeper emotional impact. In the very least, performers need to know where the climactic points were intended to be and how the composer has created those points.

Climactic rises and calming resolutions are part of every section of nearly all pieces of composed music. Music theory can help the performer discover those sections and how those movements have been created. The performer can then emphasize these things. Furthermore, every composer has some intention behind his or her work and that intention should be revealed through the music (more so for the better composer). The performer must root out that intention and see how the composer has expressed it in the music itself. In that way, the performer can then bring out these things and give his or her audience a truly moving performance.

A deeper understanding of a piece of music and what it is intended to do as a work of art is important for all other musicians as well. Whether as a production engineer, music business manager, music theater performer, radio announcer, deejay, or any other music related profession, a complete understanding of music of different styles and periods can only be beneficial to doing great work. This is especially true of the music educator who is often called upon to be some or all of these music professionals.

How To Use This Book

Each unit includes the following:
- Subsections that describe a particular concept
- Graphics about the concept
- Recommendations for music listening
- An exercise
- Answers for the exercises in the back of the book
- A homework exercise
- A practice test

With each unit you should carefully read about the concepts

and see how they are used in the examples. Then you should practice using those concepts in the practice pages. Next, the exercise should be attempted. Try to do as much as you can before looking at the answers. Lastly, do the homework exercise.

The [*] symbol seen throughout the book is used to encourage you to find a recording of the work being discussed. Many of these works can be found on sites like YouTube or other streaming sites.

The Books

This music theory series is written in four separate books:

Book One: Fundamentals
- Defines the fundamentals of music theory from music reading to chord analysis

Book Two: Chords and Part Writing
- Expands upon the concepts learned in Book One leading to the creation of traditional four part writing.

Book Three: The Tools of Analysis
- Develops an understanding of the parameters of music and how to use them in a detailed analysis of music.

Book Four: Parametric Analysis
- Applies the tools developed in all three previous books and uses them to make a complete written analysis of music from different historical periods as well as contemporary music and music from other cultures.

Each of these works were originally created as online textbooks and can be found at http://www.langermusictheory.com.

Unit One

The Basics of Rhythm

Lesson 111

Parameter: Rhythm - Basic Rhythmic Notation

Note Values - Duple Division

Filled in and open dots called notes are used to indicate which pitch is to be played and for how long. The type of note indicates the relative duration of the pitch or how long it will be played through its note value. The exact length of time is determined by something called a pulse (to be considered later). The following lists the most common note values:

Whole note, Half note, Quarter note, and Eighth note (with flag)

In the example below, notice how the whole note (measure 1), 2 half notes (measure 2), 4 quarter notes (measure 3), and 8 eighth notes (measure 4) occupy the same length of time within a measure in this example.

The whole note is an open circle. The half note adds a stem to the circle. The quarter note is a filled in circle with a stem. An eighth note can be shown with a flag or a beam.

Note values can be further divided by adding more flags or beams. For example, a note with one flag or beam is an eighth note. A note with 2 flags or beams is a 16th note, 3 flags or beams create 32nd notes, and so on. This kind of division of notes by two is called a duple division.

Rests

Just as there are moments of sound in music so there are moments of silence.

| whole rest | half rests | quarter rests | eighth rests |

These are indicated by symbols called rests and can be divided in a similar way as notes.

Exercise 111

Answer the following sentences with note or rest duration symbols.

Example: 2 eighth notes = 1 quarter note.

    1. Two quarter notes = 1 _____

    2. Two half notes = 1 _____

    3. Two eighth notes = 1 _____

    4. Two sixteenth notes = 1 _____

5. Four quarter notes = 1 _____
6. Two quarter rests = 1 _____
7. Two half rests = 1 _____
8. Two eighth rests = 1 _____
9. Two sixteenth rests = 1 _____

Homework 111

(1) How many eighth notes would equal one:
    (a) half note _____
    (b) quarter note _____
    (c) whole note _____
    (d) eighth note _____

(2) How many quarter notes would equal one:
    (a) eighth note _____
    (b) quarter note _____
    (c) half note _____
    (d) whole note _____

(3) How many sixteenth notes would equal one:
    (a) quarter note _____
    (b) whole note _____
    (c) eighth note _____
    (d) thirty-second notes _____

(4) Draw the symbol for each:
    (a) Four quarter notes = 2 _____
    (b) Eight sixteenth notes = 2 _____
    (c) Four eighth notes = 2 _____
    (d) Eight quarter notes = 2 _____
    (e) Eight quarter notes = 4 _____

(f) Four quarter notes = 8 _____
(g) Eight sixteenth notes = 4 _____
(h) Eight half notes = 4 _____
(i) Eight quarter notes = 2 _____
(j) Eight sixteenth notes = 2 _____
(k) Two whole rests = 4 _____
(l) Two half rests = 4 _____

Lesson 112

Rhythm: Ties and Dots

Ties

A tie is a curved line that connects two of the same notes together.

When two notes are "tied" the pitch is sustained through their combined values. For example, two quarter notes tied would equal the same duration as one half note.

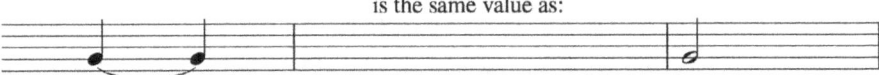

Note that a tie and a **slur** look alike but have two very different functions. Ties are always connected to the exact same notes while slurs connect different pitches. Often a tie is used to connect two notes across a bar line. Additional notes can be tied together, however.

In the above example the two whole notes are tied together across a bar line. If the whole note is equal to 4 beats in this example then the tied note would be held for 8 beats (4 beats for one whole note added to 4 beats for the second whole note).

That does not always have to be the case, however. Ties can connect any two same notes of any value together.

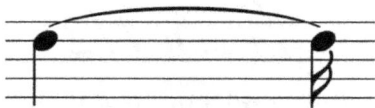

In the above example, the value of the quarter note would be added to the value of the sixteenth note.

Difference between a tie and a slur: A tie connects the same notes together to increase the rhythmic value. A slur is a line placed over different notes to indicate a connection in playing.

A slur:

Syncopation

The use of ties makes it possible to have syncopated rhythms. Syncopation occurs when a normally weak beat is emphasized. Strong beats occur when rhythms match with the pulse beat (more about pulse beats later) and weak beats are found between pulse beats. When a rhythm not on the pulse beat is emphasized then a syncopation is created.

In this example, both a dotted note and a tied note create syncopation. The second line is the pulse beat.

Syncopation is a very important rhythmic element in jazz music and the music of many non-Western cultures especially those in and around Africa.

Dots

A dot (which is actually a dot) is a symbol that extends the value of a note for 1.5 (1 and ½) times its duration. For example, a dotted whole note would equal the value of the whole note plus half the value of the whole note (the same as a half note). If the whole note had a quarter note pulse and was considered to have 4 beats then a dotted whole note would equal 6 beats (4 beats of the whole note added to 2 more beats).

In another example, a dotted quarter note would equal the value of a quarter note plus half the value of the quartet note. It would have the exact same duration as a quarter note tied to an eighth note.

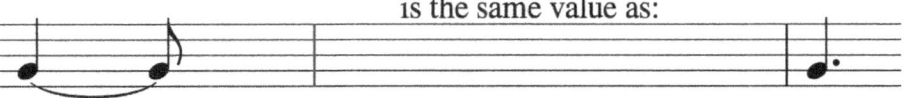

A dotted half note would equal the value of a half note plus a quarter note (half the value of the half note).

It is also possible to double or even triple dot a note.

Each dot adds another half of the value of the thing before it. In the case of a double dot, the second dot would equal half the value of the dot before it. Therefore a double dotted quarter note would have the same duration as a quarter note tied to an eighth note tied to a sixteenth note. A double dotted half note would be the same as the value of a half note tied to a quarter note tied to a quarter note.

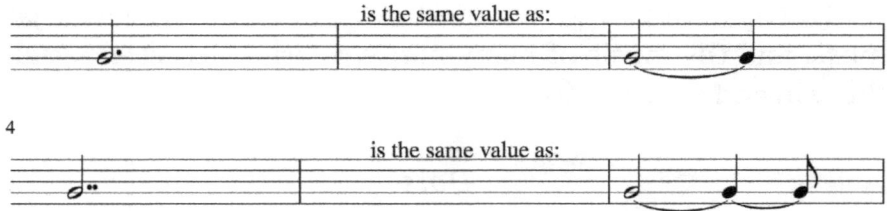

Dots can also be used with rests. Here is a dotted eighth rest.

Triple Division

With the addition of dots, notes can now have a triple division instead of duple. A dotted whole note equals three half notes. A dotted half note equals three quarter notes. A dotted quarter note equals three eighth notes, and so on.

			w.				
	h.				h.		
q.		q.		q.		q.	
e.	e.	e.	e.	e.	e.	e.	e.

Irregular Divisions

A THEORY FOR ALL MUSIC

Sometimes a line of music may include a different division. For example, a line of music in duple division may include a single beat in a triple division. When this happens it is known as an irregular division. Notes within an irregular division must include a number to tell you what that temporary division is replacing.

A quarter is usually divided into two eighth notes. An example of an irregular division of a quarter note in a duple division would be a quarter note divided into three eighth notes instead of two. This is called a triplet. The second beat in this example is a triplet marked with a 3 above it.

The 3, in this case, means 3 in the place of 2.

Here are some more examples.

Exercise 112

If the quarter note is the pulse unit, how many beats would each of the following notes receive?

1) whole note = _____

2) half note = _____

If the dotted quarter note is the pulse unit, how many beats would each of the following notes receive?

3) dotted whole note = _____

4) dotted half note = _____

If the half note is the pulse unit, how many beats would each of the following notes receive?

5) whole note = _____
6) half note = _____

Homework 112

Identify the duration of each given note.

Example: If the pulse beat is a quarter note, how many beats will there be in a half note?

Answer = 2. (The half note is equal to 2 quarter notes).

A] If the pulse is a quarter note, identify the number of beats for each:

(1) dotted whole note _____
(2) whole note _____
(3) dotted half note _____
(4) half note _____
(5) dotted quarter note _____
(6) quarter note _____
(7) eighth note _____

B] If the pulse is a dotted quarter note, identify the number of beats for each:

(1) dotted whole note _____
(2) dotted half note _____
(3) dotted quarter note _____
(4) eighth note _____

C] If the pulse is a half note, identify the number of beats for each:

(1) dotted whole note _____

(2) whole note _____

(3) dotted half note _____

(4) half note _____

(5) quarter note _____

(6) eighth note _____

Lesson 113

Rhythm: The Pulse Unit

The Pulse Unit

Many works of music have within them something called a pulse beat. The pulse beat is a consistent and even beat that underlies the music.

Imagine that you are walking down the street whistling a familiar tune. Your feet would be hitting the pavement at an even and consistent beat. Your feet are beating the pulse. The song you are whistling will have different rhythms but they will, most likely, fit within those pulses. That is how music fits within pulse beats.

Other rhythms tend to be derived and based from divisions of that pulse beat. The quarter note is the most common pulse unit in Western music for duple division music. In the following example, the second line shows the quarter note pulse beat. The upper line is a rhythm based on that pulse beat. With a quarter note pulse beat, the quarter note equals 1 beat, the half note equals 2 beats, and the whole note equals 4 beats.

From the pulse beat other rhythms are based. In this example eighth note rhythms are derived from quarter note pulses.

In triple division the dotted quarter note is often the most common pulse unit because it can be divided into three rather than two sub-units.

Any rhythmic duration can be a pulse unit including the whole note, half note, quarter note, and eighth note.

The Back Beat

Much of the contemporary music style includes a secondary pulse called the "back beat" which is usually done on beats 2 and 4 in groups of 4.

Exercise 113

Identify a most likely pulse unit for each example. See if you can feel the pulse beat and tap or clap along with it. Look for groups of notes beamed together. They often indicate pulse units.

(1)* *The Main Theme from Schindler's List*

(2)* *Pink: Just Give Me A Reason*

(3)* *Vivaldi: The Four Seasons, Summer*

(4)* *Genesis: Firth of Fifth*

Homework 113

What is the pulse unit for each?

(1)* *Vince Guaraldi: The "Peanuts" Theme*

(2) * *Christina Perri: A Thousand Years*

(3) * *Nick Drake: River Man*

(4) * *any music from the Balkans*

(5) * *Bernstein: "America" from West Side Story*

Lesson 114

Rhythm: Beaming

Definition

Beams are horizontal lines drawn to connect several notes according to the given pulse unit.

In Lesson One it was mentioned that eighth notes and smaller notes can have either flags or beams. Often these notes are beamed together to show groups of notes. When they are beamed, they are grouped within the pulse unit.

In the following example, the quarter note is the pulse unit and the two eighth notes, the triplet, and the four sixteenth notes are all beamed to show quarter note groupings.

Principles for Beaming

- Notes that do not have flags such as quarter notes or longer cannot be beamed.
- Notes must be beamed within a pulse unit and not across pulse units.
- Beams can span across rests.
- Stems in a beam usually go in the same direction together (up or down).
- Beams should not be angled more than about two notes high and stems of beamed notes should be extended to accommodate this principle.

Notice how the principles of beaming are applied in the following example.

Exercise 114

Beam notes together according to the pulse unit.

<u>Steps for doing this exercise:</u>

1. Identify the pulse unit.
2. Circle the notes within each pulse unit.
3. Beam the notes together that have flags within each pulse unit.
4. Do not beam notes across pulse units.

(1) Pulse Unit = Quarter Note

(2)   Pulse Unit = Quarter Note

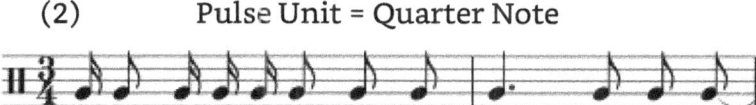

(3)   Pulse Unit = Dotted Quarter Note

(4) Pulse Unit = Dotted Quarter Note

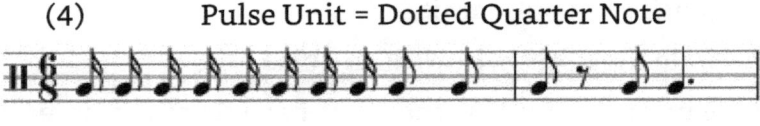

Homework 114

Beam notes according to the given pulse unit.

Lesson 115

Rhythm: Meter Signatures

Simple Meter Signatures

The pulse unit of a piece of music is often indicated at the beginning of a musical line in a device called the meter signature or time signature. The following example contains a 4/4 meter signature, a "Common Time" signature (which is the same as a 4/4 meter), a 2/2 signature, a "Cut Time" meter (which is the same as a 2/2 meter), a 2/4, 3/4, and 6/8 meter.

As you can see, the meter signature has two numbers. The bottom number indicates the pulse unit and the top number indicates how many pulse units will be in each measure until the piece ends or a new time signature is introduced.

<u>Pulse Unit Numbers</u>
1 = Whole Note
2 = Half Note
4 = Quarter Note
8 = Eighth Note
16 = Sixteenth Note

A time signature of 4/4 would mean that each measure would have 4 (the upper number) quarter note (the bottom number) pulses. All the rhythms used in the music will be based upon those four pulses. In the following example, the time signature is 3/4. The rhythms that follow fit within three quarter note pulses in each measure. Notice in measure 1 that sometimes two or more pulses can be beamed together to limit the amount of beaming. *Bach: Minuet in G Major.*

Time signatures like 2/2, 4/2, 2/4, 4/4, and 3/4 are called simple meters because their pulses have a duple division.

Compound Meters

Time signatures with pulses that have more than one pulse with a triple division like 6/8, 9/8, or 12/8 are called compound meters because they have both a duple and triple feel to them. In 6/8, for example, Every set of three eighth notes has a triple division feel to it:

1 2 3   4 5 6   1 2 3   4 5 6
(1) (2) (3) (1) (2) (3) (1) (2) (3) (1) (2) (3)

But, if the speed of the music is fast enough, groupings of three will begin to sound like one unit and a duple effect will be created (shown in parentheses).

1 2 3 4 5 6   1 2 3 4 5 6
(1)   (2)   (1)   (2)

This triple division of a duple pulse is the reason these time signatures are called compound meters. * *Beethoven: Rondo in C.*

Odd Meters

Odd meter signatures are those that have groupings of 5, 7, or 11 pulses within each measure. Examples of these include 5/4, 7/8, 7/4, 11/4, etc.

Examples:
A] * *Straight to my Heart* - Sting = 5/4.
B] * *Take Five* – Dave Brubeck = 5/4.
C} * *Money* – Pink Floyd = 7/4.

Exercise 115

Determine a meter signature for each example (more than one is possible).

A]

B]

C]

D]

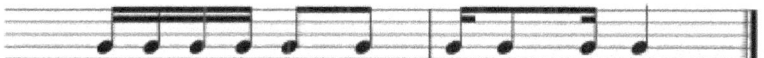

Homework 115

Determine the meter signature for each line.

1

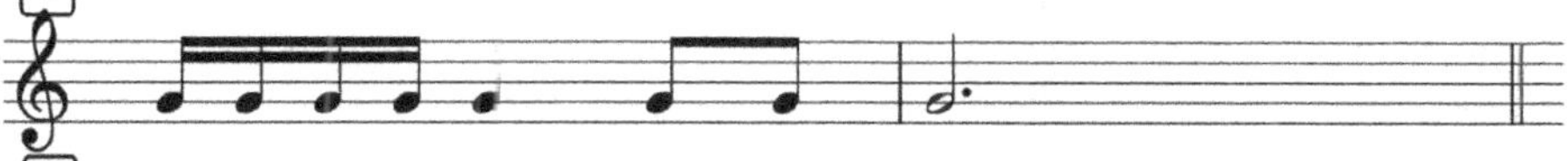

2

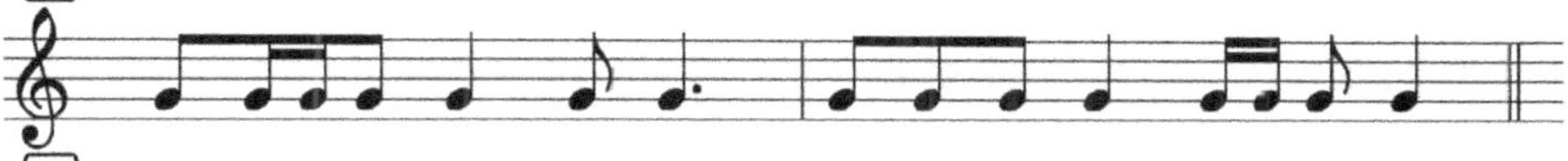

3

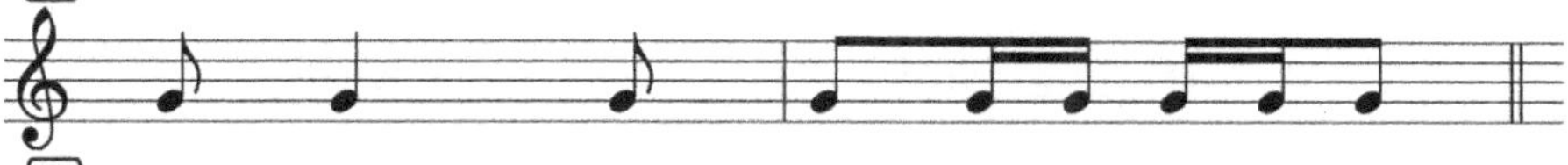

4

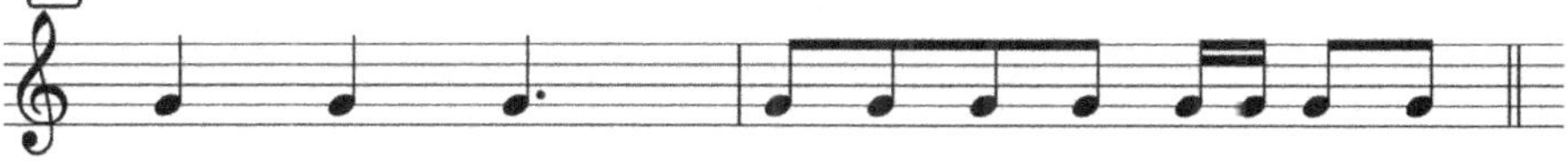

5

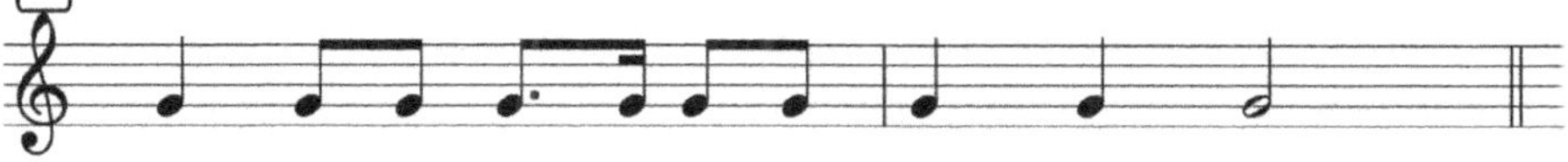

6

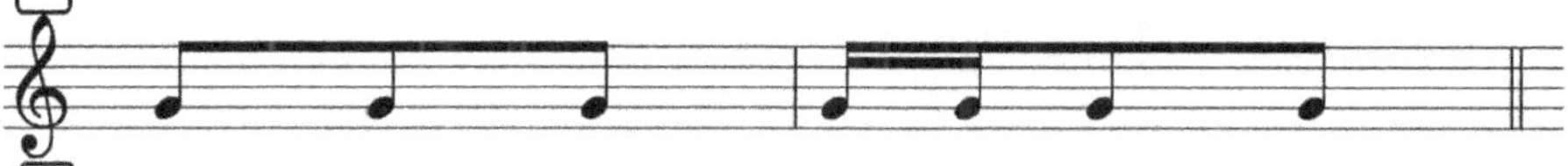

7

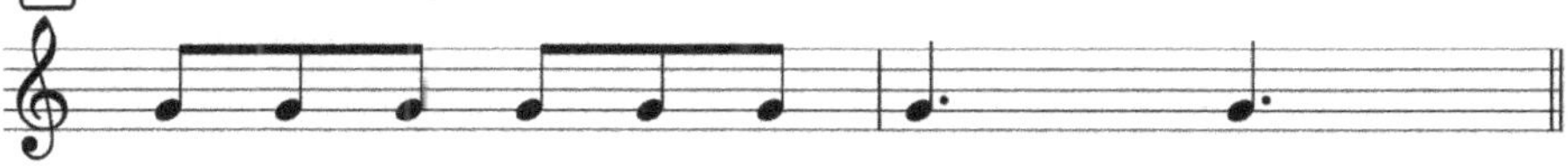

Unit One Practice Test

A] Provide rests or duration symbols for each. For example, 2

eighth notes = 1 quarter note symbol.

    (1) Two quarter rests = 1 _____
    (2) Two half rests = 1 _____
    (3) Two eighth notes = 1 _____
    (4) Two quarter notes = 1 _____
    (5) Two half notes = 1 _____
    (6) Eight sixteenth notes = 2 _____
    (7) Four quarter notes = 2 _____
    (8) Four quarter rests = 2 _____

B] Identify the duration of each note.

    (1) If the pulse is a <u>quarter note</u>, what is the duration of a:
        (a) A dotted half note = _____ beats.
        (b) A whole note = _____ beats.
    (2) If the pulse is a <u>dotted quarter note</u>, what is the duration of a:
        (a) A dotted half note = _____ beats.
        (b) A dotted whole note = _____ beats.

    (3) Beam according to the given pulse unit.

(1) Pulse unit = quarter note

(2) Pulse unit = dotted quarter note

D] Determine a meter signature for each.

Unit Two
The Basics of Pitch

Lesson 121

Melody: Pitches and Clefs

The Musical Staff

Music in Western cultures is written on a graph called a musical staff. The staff has five lines and four spaces.

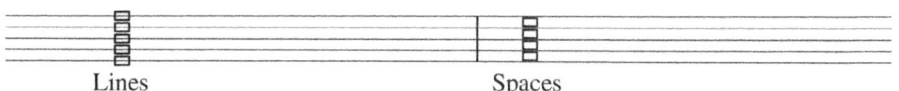

Additional lines can be added if needed. These are short lines placed above or below the staff and are called ledger lines.

ledger lines

Pitches

Pitches are depicted as being higher going up the staff and lower moving down the staff and can be shown on both the lines and the spaces of the staff.

Up

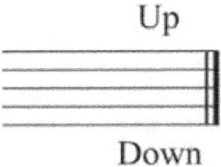

Down

The following example illustrates notes going up.

Notes On The Keyboard

Before we continue it might be helpful to learn the names of the notes that are used in a standard keyboard instrument such as a piano. The clefs are based upon notes found in different parts of the keyboard range.

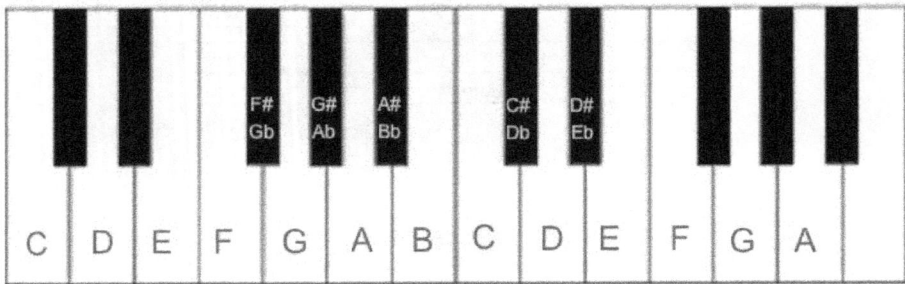

Notice the black keys. They form a particular pattern that makes it possible to find notes on the keyboard. For example, the note C is always the key just to the left of the paired black keys.

Middle C is so named because it is the C in the middle of the keyboard.

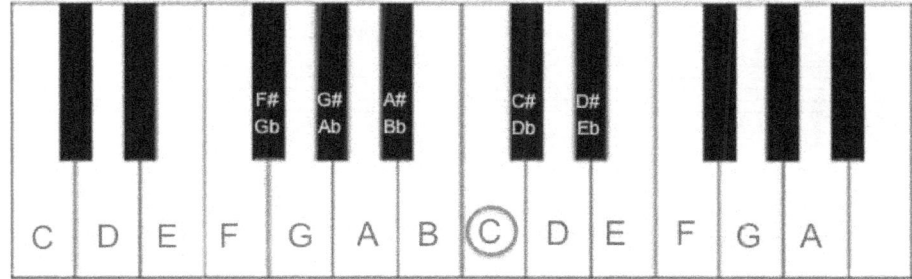

The Clefs

Specific pitches are determined by the clefs. There are three main clefs: The Treble or G clef, the Bass or F clef and the Movable or C clef.

The Treble Clef

The Treble or G clef is so named because it tends to indicate notes on the higher end (to the right of Middle C on the keyboard) and because it indicates the position of the note G. The spiral at the bottom of the clef circles the note named G.

In music, only the letters A, B, C, D, E, F, and G are used to indicate note names. If you look again at the keyboard above you will see that the note names go from A to G and then start over again. Using those seven letters, pitches on the staff are given note names.

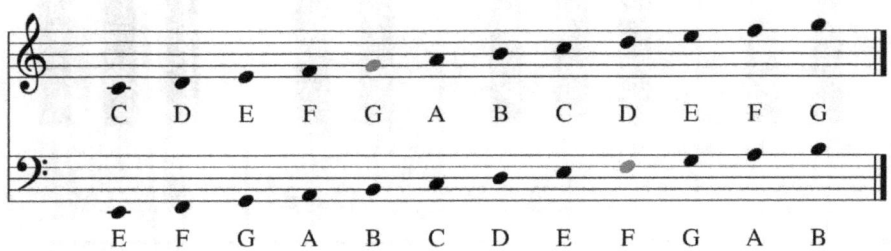

The Bass Clef

The Bass or F clef is so named because it tends to indicate notes on the lower end (to the left of middle C on the keyboard) and because it indicates the position of the note F. The spiral on the left and the two dots all encircle the position of the note F.

Notice in the above example that the names of the notes in the Bass clef are different from the names of the notes in the Treble clef.

The Grand Staff

The Grand Staff combines the Treble Clef and the Bass Clef with middle C in the middle between them.

The Grand Staff

Middle C

The Movable Clef

The movable clef is so named because it can be found in different positions. It is also called the C clef because the middle indentation identifies middle C (C4).

The note in the middle of the clef is always middle C no matter where it appears (usually on a staff line).

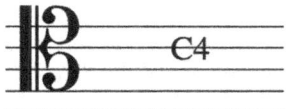

Just as with the other clefs, notes are identified up and down from the middle C location.

The FACE Method

One way to remember note names is to memorize where the note names that spell the word FACE are located in each clef.

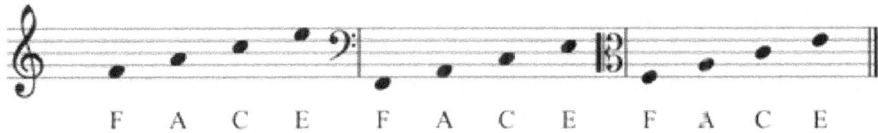

Exercise 121

Identify the note name in each clef.

Homework 121

Identify each note by clef.

Lesson 122

Melody: More On Pitches

Basic Intervals

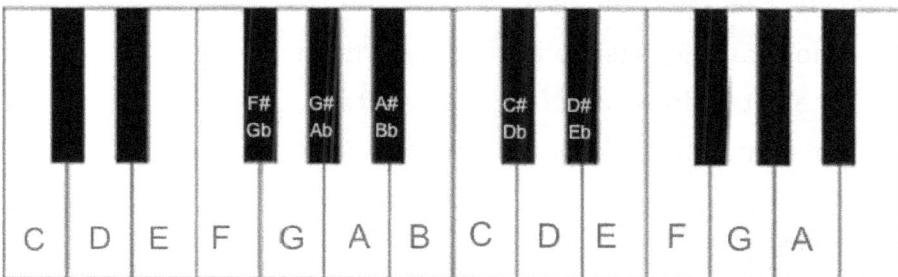

Any two keys that are directly adjacent to each other are a half step or semitone apart. Notice on the keyboard above that E and F are next to each other on the keyboard with no black key between. The distance from the note E to the note F is a semitone.

The distance between the notes F and G, however, is not a semitone because there is a black key between them (the key marked Gb). The distance from the white key F to the black key Gb is a semitone and the distance from the black key Gb to the white key G is also a semitone. Two semitones makes a whole tone so the distance from F to G is a whole tone because there is a note between them. The following two notes create a whole tone interval. (refer to the keyboard to understand why.)

Accidentals

Accidentals are symbols added to notes to change them.

The sharp (#) raises a note by a semitone.

The flat (b) lowers a note by a semitone.

A natural returns a note back to its original pitch.

The following example shows (in order) a B flat, a B natural, and a B sharp.

Using the keyboard above, the B# is the note one semitone above B which is the same as C, the Bb is the note one semitone below B or the black key between A and B, and The B natural would return the note back to the original B.

Other accidentals (shown below in order) include the double sharp (x) that raises a note two semitones and the double flat (bb) that lowers a note two semitones.

Principles for accidentals (not in key signatures):

1. Accidentals are relevant for each measure but are ignored in a new measure.
2. A natural must be used to return a note to its original pitch in the same measure.

3. A courtesy accidental (an accidental in parentheses) can be used to remind a player whether or not a note has been changed or returned.

Enharmonics

An enharmonic is when two notes with different names appear to be the same note on the keyboard. Look at the keyboard below. The note F# (the black key just above F) and the note Gb (the black key just below G) appear as the same note.

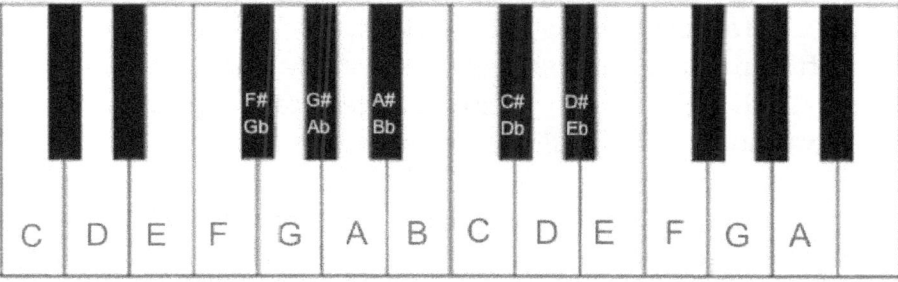

Another example: the note Fx (F double sharp) and Abb (A double flat) are also enharmonics. Both would appear to be the same note, G on the keyboard.

Note: I say "appear to be" because sometimes they are not actually the same note. On a keyboard, F# and Gb are the same notes because keyboard instruments have fixed intonations—they cannot alter the tuning of individual notes. In other instruments such as string instruments, air-blown instruments, and the voice, which can alter the tuning of individual notes, F# and Gb would not be performed exactly the same. An F# would be played slightly higher than a Gb. That is because sharped notes are usually on their way up to the next pitch and flatted notes are usually on their way down.

Note: In music theory questions, sometimes two notes may be enharmonics but one note will be the correct answer while the other note will not. Changing a note to its enharmonic changes the interval. For example, C to D# is a 2nd while C to Eb is a 3rd.

Octave Identifications

An octave is another special interval. Octaves are notes that are 8 notes apart on the keyboard and which share the same letter name. On the keyboard above notice that the third note in on the left is a C. Seven notes up the keyboard you find another C. The interval from C to C is called an octave (from the word for eight). Notes at a specific octave are identified with a number. Middle C, for example, is called C4 because it is the 4th C from the left found on a standard keyboard. If you know where middle C is in each clef, you can figure out the octave number of every note by counting up or down from C4. Remember that musical notes only go from A to G and then start over again. In the next chart, observe the notes shown at the top and the octave numbers shown in the last row just above the keyboard. The 8va symbol means to play the notes an octave above. Though not shown here an 8vb symbol would mean to play the notes an octave below.

In the following example, the notes from top to bottom would be called C2, C3, C4 (middle C), C3, and C2.

Sometimes it is necessary to indicate that notes written should be played an octave above or below the note. This is often done with an 8va (octave above) or 8vb (octave below) designation.

Exercise 122

Identify the note given by name and octave identification then write an enharmonic for it. The first one has been done for you.

<u>Steps for doing this exercise:</u>

    1. Identify the note given with accidental (if added).

    2. Write the note name with octave number underneath.

    3. Provide an enharmonic next to it (use keyboard, if needed).

Homework 122

Identify the note with octave numbers.

KENNETH P. LANGER

Lesson 123

Texture: Basic Concepts

Macro Dynamics

Dynamics are levels of volume or loudness and softness. Dynamics can happen on a macro and a micro level. Macro dynamics can happen for an entire piece of music but, more often, dynamics happen within different sections of a work of music. Dynamics can range from very loud to very soft. In classical music there are particular terms used to indicate relative levels of volume.

Piano (P) means to play the music soft. Forte (F) (pronounced for-tay) means to play the music loud. Mezzo (M) (pronounced met-so) means moderately so a Mezzopiano (MP) means moderately soft and a Mezzoforte (MF) means moderately loud.

The following shows the dynamics: piano, mezzopiano, mezzoforte, and forte.

Doubled letters mean more, so double Forte - called a fortissimo - means very loud.

A double piano - called a pianissimo - means very soft.

The following chart gives a relative basis for each of the basic dynamics.

Dynamic	Comparison
PP	a whisper
P	between speaking and a whisper
MP	soft speaking voice
MF	loud speaking voice
F	a drill sergeant's voice
FF	yelling

Additional dynamics can be created by adding more letters to the FF or PP. For example, an FFF would mean to play the music louder than Fortissimo.

Dynamics can also be indicated to change over time.

A crescendo (cresc.) means to get gradually louder.

A decrescendo (decresc.) or diminuendo (dim.) means to get gradually softer.

A THEORY FOR ALL MUSIC

Classical music can also use a lot of foreign language words to indicate changes in dynamics and other things. You should always look those up before performing such a work.

Micro Dynamics (Articulations)

Dynamics can also change at the level of every note. Notes can be marked with small accents or sforzando marks to make them start loud and get immediately softer to create an "attacked" note. Here is a small sample of accent marks.

The staccato is a dote placed above a note and means to play the note short while a legato is a line above the note and means to play it long.

The Sforzando

A similar effect is created with the Fortepiano mark.

Both mean to attack the note loudly then release it.

Shaping specific notes can be done with marks called articulations. Below are some common articulations with a chart describing them.

47

No.	Name	Description
1	Staccato	Played short with silence after
2	Staccatissimo	Even shorter than the Staccato
3	Marcato	Played forcefully with some space
4	Accent	Played with a hard attack then soft
5	Legato	Played long with very little space between notes

Tempo Markings

Tempo markings determine the speed of the music. Sometimes an exact measurement of tempo is used with a metronome marking (MM). A metronome measures the number of beats per minute.

A metronome marking of quarter = 120 means that the quarter note pulse should go by at 120 beats per minute.

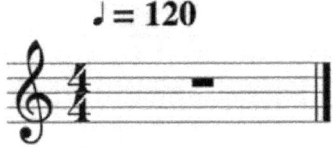

Classical music uses some terms to indicate relative tempos. Below is a chart with classical terms, their relative definition and an approximate BPM equivalent. There are several variations and gradations of all of these but these are the basic ones.

Name	Contemporary Equivalent	Relative Speed	Metronome Equivalent
Grave		very slow	+/- 30 BPM
Lento		slow	+/- 40 BPM
Largo		broadly	+/- 50 BPM
Adagio	slow ballad	stately	+/- 60 BPM
Andante	medium ballad	walking pace	+/- 70 BPM
Moderato	funk	moderately	+/- 90 BPM
Allegro	rock	fast	+/- 110 BPM
Vivace	house/techno	lively	+/- 135 BPM
Presto	speed metal	very fast	+/- 150 BPM

Tempos can also be changed over time. The two most common ways are through the ritardando and the accelerando.

- Ritardando (rit.) means to gradually get slower.
- The Accelerando (accel.) means to gradually get faster.

There are many more terms that can be used to change tempo.

Exercise 123

A] Provide a symbol and an explanation for each:

For example: piano

   symbol: p

   explanation: means to play the music soft

1. Forte
2. Mezzopiano

3. Crescendo
4. Sforzando
5. Staccato
6. Andante
7. Ritardando

B] Identify marks in the following piece. Describe whether it is a tempo marking, a dynamic marking, or an articulation and what it means. * *Webern: Four Pieces for Violin and Piano, no. 1.*

Homework 123

A] Give the symbol and the definition for each:

1. Piano
2. Mezzo Piano
3. Fortissimo

4. Mezzo Forte
5. Forte
6. Pianissimo
7. Crescendo
8. Decrescendo
9. Fortepiano
10. Sforzando
11. Staccato
12. Legato
13. Marcato
14. Accent

B] Give a relative speed for each:

1. Vivace
2. Grave
3. Largo
4. Moderato
5. Andante
6. Allegro

Lesson 124

Melody: The Major Scale

Definition of a Scale

A musical scale is a set of notes usually within an octave. The octave beginning and end notes are usually the fundamental pitch for that scale. The notes within that scale form a series of intervals (often whole tones and semitones). Those exact intervals define the scale. The scale acts as a kind of pitch catalog from which compositions are based.

Many scales use the same notes both ascending and descending but some use different notes.
Some Scales

Here are some examples of different scales.

(1) The Chromatic Scale - a scale based on semitones.

(2) The Whole Tone Scale - a scale based on whole tones.

(3) The Pentatonic or five tone scale.

(4) A closely related scale used a lot in jazz and contemporary music is the Blues Scale. There are several forms of the blues scale. This one is called the minor pentatonic form.

(5) The Octatonic or Diminished Scale

(6) An Arabic Scale

(7) An example of an Indian Raga (Bhimpalazi):

Note: Indian Ragas are very different from Western scales. The notes above are an approximation of the actual raga. Indian ragas are very complex and include practices for including microtones (notes between semitones) and the use of other notes under special circumstances.

The Major Scale

Two scales predominate the tonal system of music: the

major scale and the three forms of the minor scale. The major scale has a specific set of whole steps and half. In the example below, the whole steps are marked with curved lines and the half steps are marked with straight lines. Notice the scale is mostly whole steps with half steps between notes 3-4 and 7-8. A major scale must have these exact intervals.

Since the scale begins and ends on C (the central pitch) it is based on that note and the scale is called the C major scale.

To construct a major scale, you would begin with the central pitch and work upwards selecting the notes at the proper intervals. Use a piano keyboard to see which intervals are whole steps and half steps.

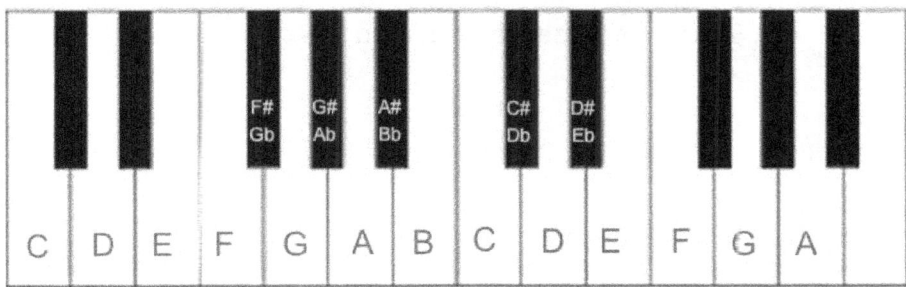

Scale Degree Names

In the C major scale, the C is called the tonic pitch and each pitch is named in relation to it.

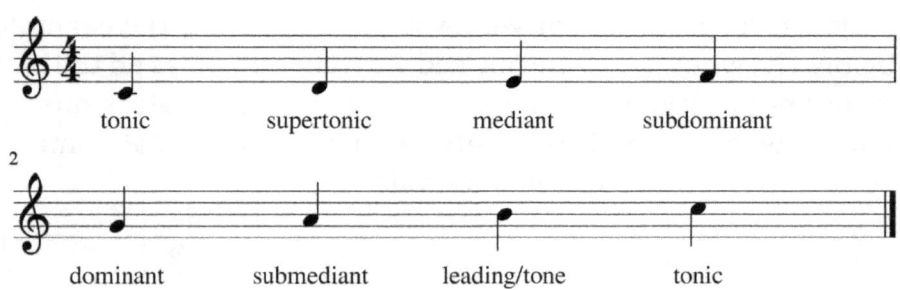

Exercise 124

Steps for doing this exercise:

1. Draw notes between the octave (leave space for accidentals).
2. Mark where whole and half steps should go.
3. Start from the bottom and check intervals (change when needed).

Build a major scale on a musical staff based on the following notes:

(a) G
(b) B
(c) Eb
(d) Bb

Homework 124

Write a major scale starting with each of the following notes.

A THEORY FOR ALL MUSIC

Lesson 125

Melody: The Minor Scales

The Natural Minor Scale

The minor scale is the other of the two main scales of the tonal system. Like the major scale, the minor scale is a specific set of whole steps and half steps. Unlike the major scale the minor scale has three different forms. We will first consider the natural minor scale. Here is the natural minor scale starting on A.

Notice that the half steps are in different places compared to the major scale. The half steps in the major scale are between steps 3-4 and 7-8 while the half steps in the natural minor scale are between steps 2-3 and 5-6. It can be constructed in the same way.

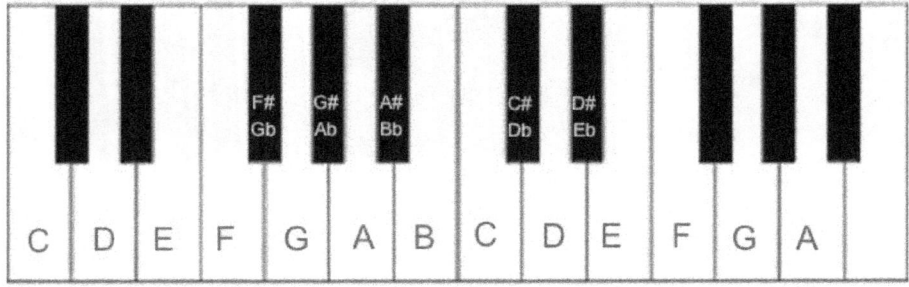

The Harmonic Minor Scale

The harmonic minor scale is a variation on the natural minor scale. It contains the same notes with one difference: the seventh scale degree is raised a semitone. The harmonic minor scale is so named because composers like to use these notes when harmonizing in minor keys. When building chords, they like the sound of the leading tone being closer to the tonic.

Compare the natural minor scale with the harmonic minor scale below.

The A harmonic minor scale: ascending and descending

The notes of the A natural harmonic minor scale are:

A, B, C, D, E, F, G, A

The seventh note above A is G.

In the A harmonic minor scale the G is changed to G#.

The Melodic Minor Scale

The melodic minor scale is yet another variation on the natural minor scale. In this scale the notes ascending are different from the notes descending. From the natural minor scale the 6th and 7th scale degrees are raised going up the scale but they are returned to their original pitches when coming down. The melodic minor scale is so named because composers like to use the raised 6th and 7th notes in melodic lines that are rising or going up towards tonic but keep the natural minor

6th and 7th notes when the melody is coming down so that the sound of the minor scale is maintained. Compare the A natural minor scale to the A melodic minor scale.

The A natural minor scale:

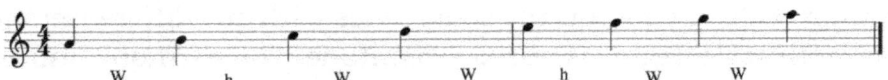

The A melodic minor scale: ascending and descending

Sometimes in Jazz music, the raised 6th and 7th scale degrees of the melodic minor scale are used in both ascending and descending forms.

Exercise 125

Write out the following minor scales:

1. D natural minor

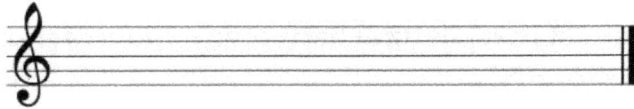

2. G natural minor

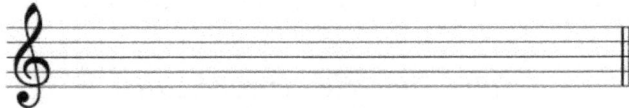

3. D harmonic minor

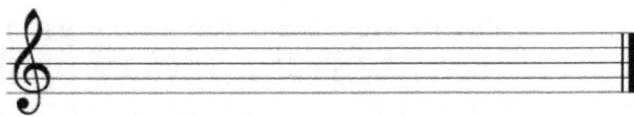

4. B harmonic minor

5. E melodic minor

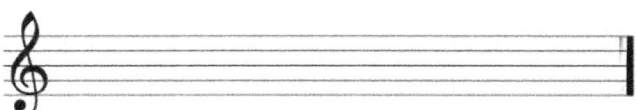

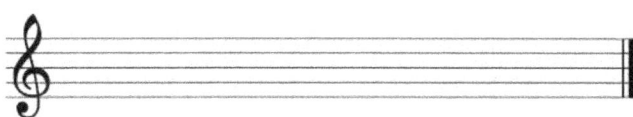

Homework 125

Write the following minor scales on the notes given.

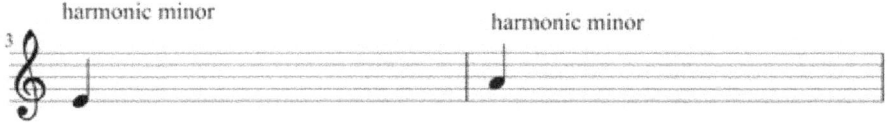

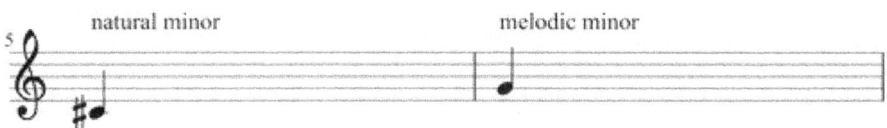

Unit Two Practice Test

A] Identify each note by name and octave number.

B] Write the following scales.

A THEORY FOR ALL MUSIC

53

Unit Three
Key Signatures

Lesson 131

Parameter: Melody-Key Signatures

Definition

Imagine that someone decides to write a piece of music based on the E major scale. The E major scale has four sharped notes in it: F#, C#, G#, and D#. Every single time that composer put in any of those four notes each would have to have a sharp added to it. It can get tedious writing all those sharps and the score can get a bit messy so composers came up with a short cut to tell performers that certain notes were to have accidentals throughout some or all of a musical work. In our current example, this method of short hand would tell the performer that every time a F, C, G, or D was encountered it should be played with a sharp. That method of shorthand is called the Key Signature. The key signature is a set of sharps or flats placed at the beginning of a work of music that tells which notes should be altered throughout or until the next key signature is encountered.

Consider the following piece that uses the scale of C minor which has three flats in its natural form: Bb, Eb, and Ab. Each time these notes come up (and notes related to the other forms of the minor scale as well), a flat must be added to the note. * *Bach: Prelude in C Minor.*

Look at the same piece now using a key signature.

A THEORY FOR ALL MUSIC

Major Key Signatures

A key signature places accidentals at the beginning of the music. The key signature for E major places the four sharps that make up the E major scale at the beginning. The following example shows a grand staff and the key signature for E major in both treble and bass clefs.

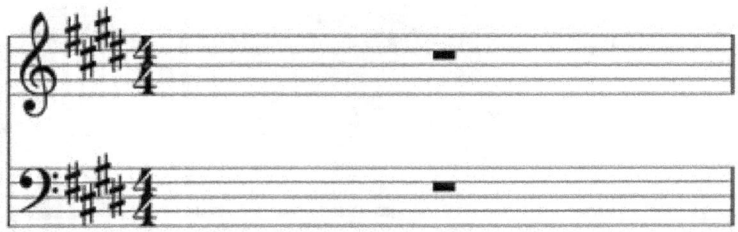

Here are some more examples of major key signatures based on the scales constructed in the unit on major scales.

The G major scale:

The key signature of G major:

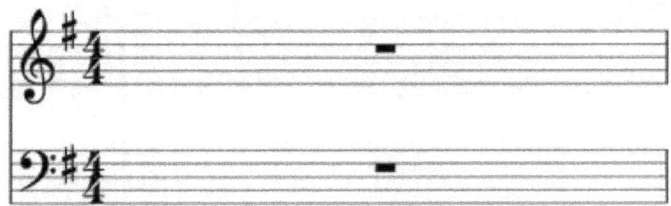

The B major scale:

The key signature of B major:

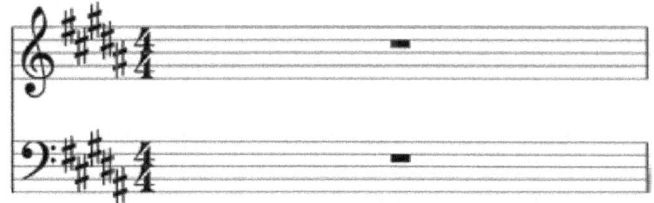

The Eb major scale:

The key signature of Eb major:

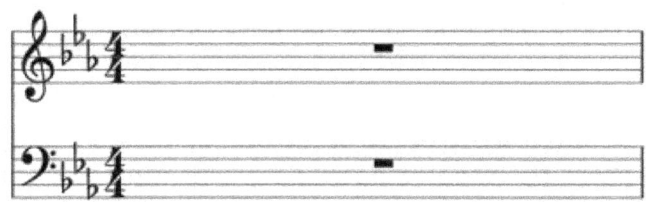

The Bb major scale

The key signature of Bb major:

The Placement of Sharps and Flats

It is important that performers be able to quickly recognize what key they are in. To make identification easy, the sharps and flats in key signatures are put into specific places and in a specific order.

Look at the examples above again. Notice that the key signatures with sharps start with the same sharp (F#) each time and the sharps are placed in exactly the same way. The same is true for the key signatures with flats. They also always start with the same flat (Bb) and place the flats exactly the same way each time.

You can remember the order of sharps by memorizing seven letters. I call these the Seven Magic Letters because they can help with several different musical concepts.

The Seven Magic Letters

F C G D A E B

These seven letters are the order of all the sharps for all the key signatures. Notice the key signature of C# major. It contains all seven sharps in the proper order and placement.

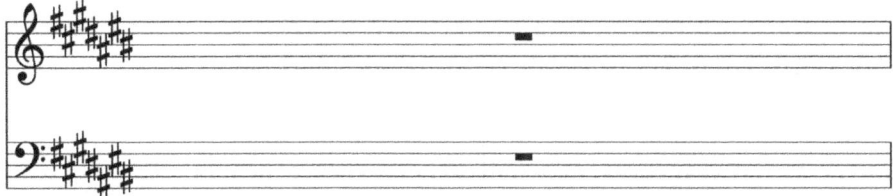

Notice that the sharps appear in their order and that they start up high and then zig-zag up and down alternatively (except for A because that would require adding a ledger line).

There is also an order to the flats but if you know the Seven Magic Letters then you already know the order of flats because the order of flats is the reverse of the order of sharps. The order of the flats is BEADGCF. Notice the key signature of Cb major. It contains all seven flats in the proper order and placement.

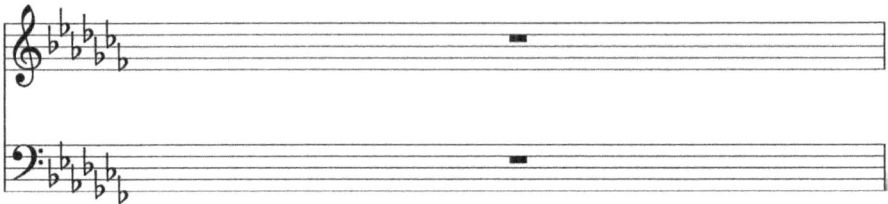

Flats start low and then zig-zag up and down.

Creating a Major Key Signature

To create a key signature in any given major key, do the following:

1. Determine the key
2. Determine the number of flats or sharps needed
3. Put the sharps or flats in the proper order and placement

To determine the number of sharps of flats in a key you can use the same seven magic letters.

The Seven Magic Letters	F	C	G	D	A	E	B
The number of sharps:		0	1	2	3	4	5

Of course, this does not give us all seven sharps. To get there you simply repeat the same seven letters with #s added.

Major Keys:	F	C	G	D	A	E	B
Sharps:		0	1	2	3	4	5
Major Keys:	F#	C#					
Sharps:	6	7					

The same method can be used to find the number of flats.

Major Key:		Cb	Gb	Db	Ab	Eb	Bb
Accidentals:		7b	6b	5b	4b	3b	2b
Major Key:	F	C	G	D	A	E	B
Accidentals:	1b	0	1#	2#	3#	4#	5#
Major Key:	F#	C#					
Accidentals:	6#	7#					

Notice that sharps increase as you go to the right in the chart from C major and flats increase as you go to the left of C major.

Once you know the number of sharps or flats in a given key you can construct the key signature by placing the accidentals in the proper placement and order.

You can also use the same chart to determine the name of a key signature by counting the number of sharps or flats and then see which major key signature has that number.

Keep in mind, however, that the fastest and most efficient

way to learn and use key signatures is to memorize them. Use flashcards or a practice site to memorize key signatures until you know them well. Start with keys with 1 flat and 1 sharp then gradually add sharps and flats.

Exercise 131

(1) Construct the following key signatures in treble and bass clefs.

   (a) D major

   (b) F# major

   (c) Ab major

   (d) Bb major

Steps for doing this exercise

- Determine whether the key has sharps or flats.
- Determine how many sharps or flats.
- Place those in proper sequence and placement

(2) Identify the following key signatures.

A)

B)

Homework 131

A] **Provide the following major key signatures.**

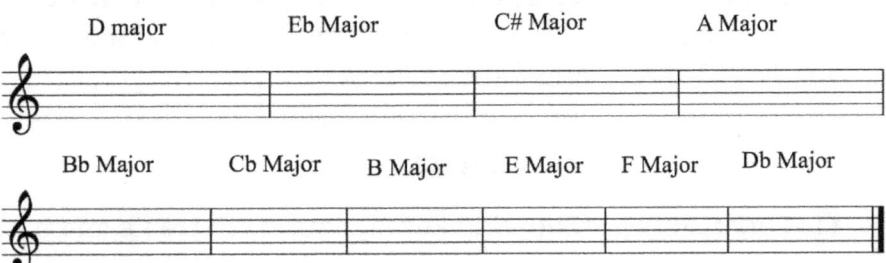

B] **Identify the following major key signatures.**

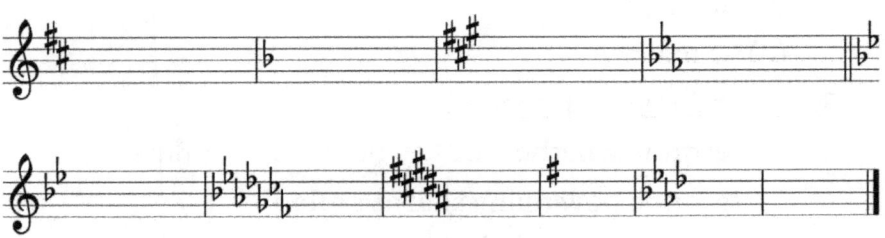

Lesson 132

Melody: Minor Key Signatures

Construction

Just as with major scales, the use of minor scales creates the need for minor key signatures. For the major scales, additions of sharps and flats to the key signature in the order of flats and sharps developed upwards and downwards from C major - the major key with no sharps and flats. The same thing can be done with minor key signatures with one change. Instead of starting at C, minors begin at the key of A because the key of A minor has no sharps or flats. With that in mind you can use the same chart as the majors but with 0 placed at A.

Minor Key:					Ab	Eb	Bb
Accidentals:					7b	6b	5b
Minor Key:	F	C	G	D	A	E	B
Accidentals:	4b	3b	2b	1b	0	1#	2#
Minor Key:	F#	C#	G#	D#	A#		
Accidentals:	3#	4#	5#	6#	7#		

Another way to find a minor key signature is to add three flats to the major.

<u>C major = 0 flats, C minor = 3 flats</u>

Compare the major key signatures to the minor.

	F	C	G	D	A	E	B
Major key:	1b	0	1#	2#	3#	4#	5#
Minor Key:	4b	3b	2b	1b	0	1#	2#

Relative Key Relationships

Major and minor key signatures have some unique relationships. For example the key signature of C major and A minor are related because they both have the same number of sharps and flats (none). When a major and a minor key signature share the same number of accidentals it is called a relative key relationship.

Think of it this way: If you share your keys with a family member in your house, you and your relatives share the same keys.

Relative Key Signatures

Sharps	0	1	2	3	4	5	6	7
Major Key	C	G	D	A	E	B	F#	C#
Minor Key	A	E	B	F#	C#	G#	D#	A#

Flats	0	1	2	3	4	5	6	7
Major Key	C	F	Bb	Eb	Ab	Db	Gb	Cb
Minor Key	A	D	G	C	F	Bb	Eb	Ab

Notice that in each case above, the relative minor key is three half steps below its major key:

<u>major key: C - (B) - (Bb) - relative minor key A</u>

Parallel Key Relationships

When two keys have the same letter name such as C major and C minor, they have a <u>parallel</u> key relationship. Think of it this way: you might have a family member that no longer wants to live at home but wants to live nearby - like on a parallel street. You may share similar names but not the same keys.

Some Parallel Key Signatures

Major Key	C (0)	D (2#)	Eb (3b)	G (1#)	A (3#)	Bb (2b)
Minor Key	C (3b)	D (1b)	Eb (6b)	G (2b)	A (C)	Bb (5b)

Changing Major to Minor

Another interesting relationship between parallel major and minor keys is that a major key can be changed into a minor key by adding 3 flats (and vice versa). Look at the chart above. The key of C major can be changed into the key of C minor by adding three flats - the first three flats in the order of flats (Bb, Eb, Ab).

In the next column, the key signature of D major has two sharps. If you add three flats to it, the first two are cancelled out and one remains so the key signature of D minor has 1 flat.

Key Signature of D major

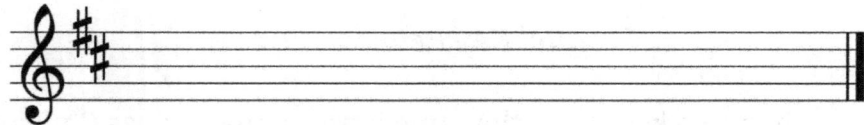

Key Signature of D minor

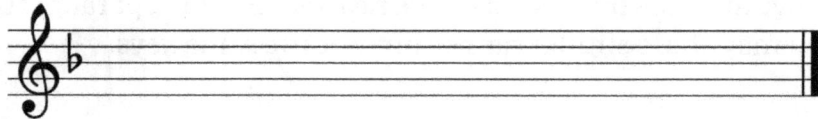

Exercise 132

(1) Construct the following key signatures:
- (a) Bb minor
- (b) G# minor
- (c) F minor
- (d) F# minor

(2) Identify the following minor key signatures
- (a)

- (b)

Homework 132

A] Construct the following minor key signatures.

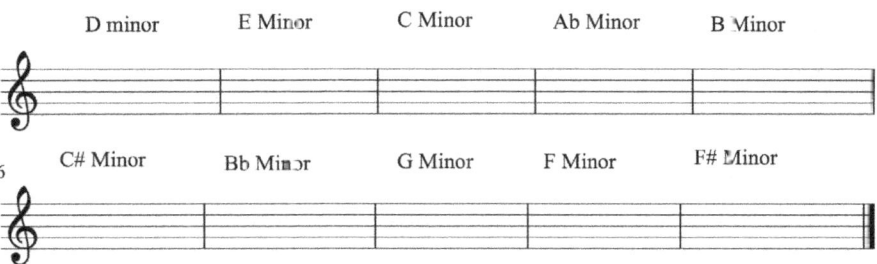

B] Identify the following minor key signatures.

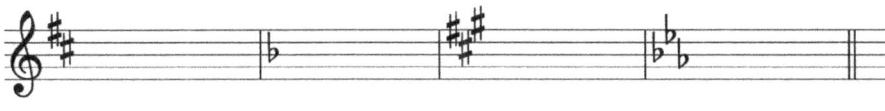

Lesson 133

Melody and Harmony: Perfect and Major Intervals

Intervals from the Major Scale

We learned that musical intervals are the distances between notes. In this unit the intervals created from the distance between the tonic of a scale and the other notes of the scale will be examined. In the following example the tonic of the scale is repeated under the notes of the scale creating intervals from that tonic note. The intervals are named by counting the number of notes between them.[change to intervals based on C major]

U stands for unison or "same note." The 8th is usually called an "octave." The interval from F to G is called a second because there is a distance of two notes, and so on. In music we count the bottom note as "1" not "0."

Interval Quality

Intervals are also named by their quality which is a more specific identification because it takes into account possible accidentals. Most of the intervals based from the major scale are called major intervals.

A THEORY FOR ALL MUSIC

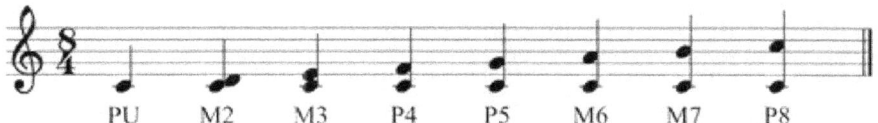

The exception to these are the unison, 4th, 5th, and 8th (octave) which are called perfect intervals. The reason for this is mostly historical but the names have remained.

When analyzing these intervals, a capital M is used for major intervals and a capital P is used for perfect intervals.

Harmonic vs. Melodic Intervals

The intervals above are all examples of harmonic intervals because they are played together. If the two notes are separated in time they are said to be melodic. In the example below the top line illustrates melodic intervals and the bottom line illustrates harmonic intervals.

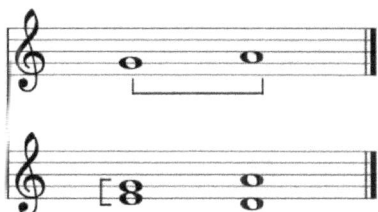

Compound Intervals

Compound intervals are those beyond the octave. For example, the next interval beyond the octave (the 8th) would be called a 9th.

Major 9th

A major 9th is the same as a major 2nd up an octave. To find the octave equivalent of a compound interval, subtract 7. For example: 9-7=2.

Major 2nd

Here are all the major and perfect intervals up two octaves with compound intervals.

Inverted Intervals

When you invert something you turn it upside down. For example, here is a question mark (?) that has been inverted.

? inverted = ¿

Musical intervals can also be inverted. When you do that, however, the distance from the bottom note to the top note is changed. The following example contains an inversion of a unison, a second, a third, a fourth, and a fifth.

Notice the result of inverting intervals:

unison	when inverted becomes	octave
2nd	when inverted becomes	7th
3rd	when inverted becomes	6th
4th	when inverted becomes	5th
5th	when inverted becomes	4th
6th	when inverted becomes	3rd
7th	when inverted becomes	2nd

The quality of the interval also changes when inverted. Notice the result of inverting intervals:

major	becomes	minor
perfect	remains	perfect

More on inverted intervals in the next unit.

Exercise 133

To do this exercise, always base the interval from the key of the lowest note and work up according to the scale degrees of that key.

For example, to find a P5 (perfect 5th) above Eb, establish the key of Eb major (3 flats: Bb, Eb, Ab) and then count up from the bottom of the Eb major scale until you come to the 5th note of the scale. Remember that tonic is 1 not 0. The answer is Bb.

Steps for doing this exercise:
- Write out the major scale or key of the root note.
- Count up the interval from the bottom note.
- (remember the root note is 1 not 0)
- Use the note from the scale or key for your answer

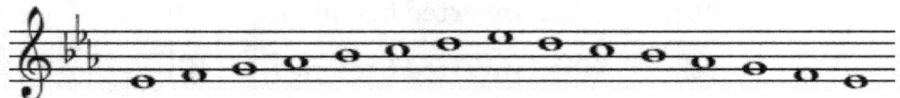

(1) Write the note that completes the following intervals:
   (a) M2 above F#
   (b) P5 above Ab
   (c) M3 above F
   (d) M6 above Bb
   (e) P4 above D
   (f) M7 above E

2) Identify the following intervals:

Steps for doing this exercise:
- Count the number of notes from the bottom note.
- Mark it as either a Major (M) or Perfect (P) interval.

a)

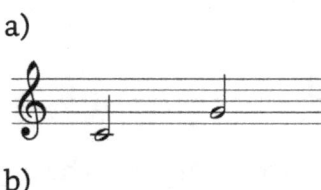

b)

c)

Homework 133

A] Provide the note that completes the following major and perfect intervals above the given note.

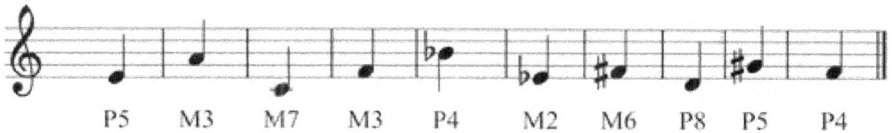

B] Identify the following major and perfect intervals.

Lesson 134

Melody and Harmony: Minor and Altered Intervals

Minor Intervals

Just as it is possible to create intervals from the major scale, the same can be done with the minor scale–almost! There is one exception, however. Look what happens when the natural minor scale is used in the following examples to create intervals.

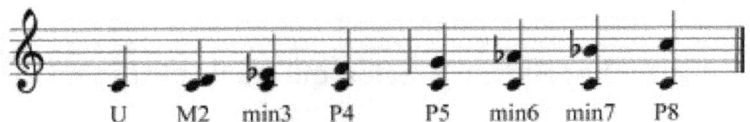

Compare the intervals in the minor scale to major and perfect intervals found in the major scale (see previous unit).

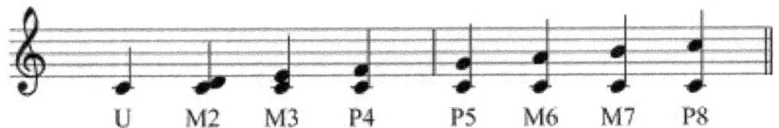

Notice "min" is used to designate a minor interval here to make a clear distinction between a minor (min) interval and a major (M) interval. Also notice that the second remains major in the minor scale.

Altering Major Intervals to Find Minor Intervals

Although the minor scale can be used to find some minor intervals you can see that not all intervals are minor in the minor scale. The more efficient way to find minor and other intervals is to alter them from the major intervals. Notice above that the Major 3rd (from the major scale) becomes a minor 3rd (from the minor scale) when lowering it one semitone.

The same is true for the 6th and the 7th. If you lower the M6 or M7 a semitone they become a min6 and min7 respectively.

Diminished Intervals

Changing a major interval into a minor one by lowering it a semitone is just one of several ways of altering intervals. If you lower a minor interval by another semitone it becomes diminished. To diminish something is to make it smaller so a diminished interval is a smaller distance than a major or perfect interval. Here is a M6 above C or the sixth scale degree of the C major scale.

If the A above is lowered one semitone the interval becomes a min6

If the Ab on top is lowered yet another semitone the interval becomes a Diminished Sixth (dim6).

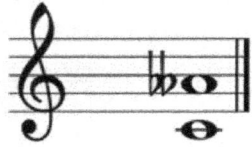

One reason that perfect intervals are different is because, when lowered, they immediately become diminished rather than minor. Here is a perfect fifth (P5) above C or the fifth scale degree of the C major scale.

If you lower the top note down a semitone the P5 becomes a Diminished fifth (dim5).

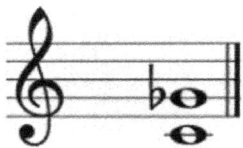

Augmented Intervals

To augment something is to make it bigger. An augmented interval has more space than a major or perfect interval. A major interval raised one semitone becomes augmented. Here is the M6 above C again.

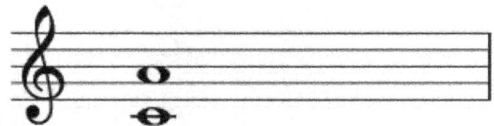

When the top note is raised a semitone the M6 becomes an

Augmented Sixth (A6).

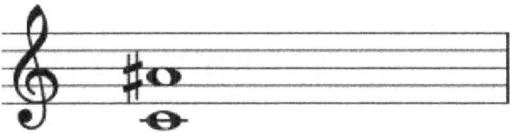

The same is true for perfect intervals. When a perfect interval is raised a semitone it becomes an augmented interval. Here, again is a perfect fifth above C.

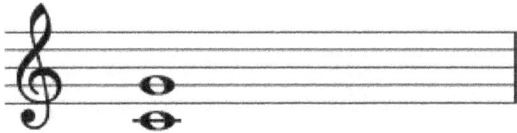

When the top note is raised a semitone the interval becomes an Augmented Fifth (A5).

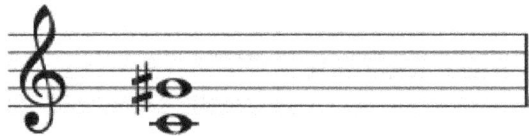

Altering Intervals Down

Intervals can also be altered by changing the bottom note rather than the top but the principle remains the same. In the following example the intervals have been changed by altering the lowest note.

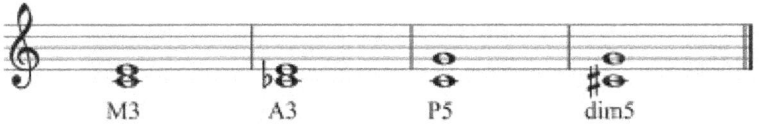

The Interval Chart

To better understand how this works it is helpful to think of the space between the notes. The following table illustrates how intervals change by altering either the top or bottom note.

Major/minor Intervals	Distance Increased	Distance Decreased
Augmented	/\	\/
Major	/\	\/
Minor	/\	\/
Diminished	/\	\/

Perfect Intervals	Distance Increased	Distance Decreased
Augmented	/\	\/
Perfect	/\	\/
Diminished	/\	\/

Combined Chart

All Intervals		
Augmented		Increase /\
Perfect	Major	
	minor	
Diminished		\/ decrease

Intervals Below

Sometimes it is necessary to find an interval below a given note. There are two ways to do this by inverting the interval and counting up or by a trail and error method.

Method 1: Inverted Intervals
- Invert the interval.
- Find the note above the inverted note.
- Move that note down an octave.

Method 2: Trial and Error
- Count down the number of notes to 1.
- Try different accidentals on that note to see which one produces the correct result.

In the above example (M6 below A), six notes below A is C. The answer must be a C "something" to call it a 6th below. The note can be either a Cbb, Cb, C, C#, or Cx. Start with C and ask if A is the sixth scale degree of the C major scale. If yes then you have found the answer. If no then alter the lower note with a different accidental to find the correct interval.

Exercise 134

(1) Provide the note for the following intervals above:
  (a) M3 above Ab
  (b) M7 above E
  (c) M2 above Bbb
  (d) M6 above Ab

(e) P5 above F#

(f) P4 above Bb

(g) A4 above C

(h) d5 above Dx

(i) min3 above D

(j) min 6 above G#

Steps for doing this exercise:
- Identify the major key signature of the bottom note.
- Count up to the scale degree number within that scale to find the major or perfect interval above.
- If the bottom note does not lend itself to an easily recognizable key signature due to accidentals. Find the answer without the accidentals then place the accidentals back into all pitches.
- Alter that interval if needed to find minor, diminished, or augmented intervals.
- TIP: all perfect intervals except B-F or F-B share the same accidentals.

(2) Provide the note for the following intervals below:
- (a) M2 below C
- (b) M7 below C#
- (c) P5 below Eb
- (d) M3 below G#
- (e) A5 below F#

Steps for doing this exercise:
Determine which method you will use to find your answer.
- Inversion method

- invert the interval
- find that note above the inverted note
- write that note down an octave
- Trial and error method
  - Count down the number of steps requested by the interval number.
  - Try different accidentals on that note to see which one fits the interval requested.

3) Identify the following intervals:

Steps for doing this exercise:
- Count up the number of notes between the bottom note and the top note.
- Identify the key signature of the bottom note.
- If the key signature is unusual:
  - Remove the accidental and find the answer without it, then
  - Replace the accidental in all notes.
- Determine whether or note the top note is in the major key signature of the bottom note.
  - If it is then the answer is a major or perfect interval.
  - If not, then notice how it has been altered and use the chart above to find your answer.

Homework 134

A] Construct the following intervals above the given notes.

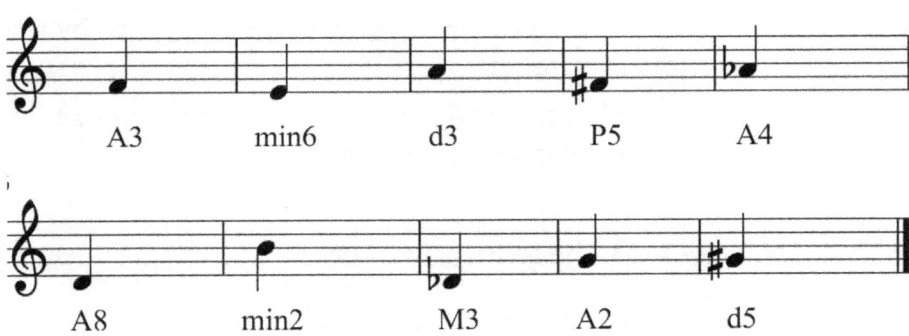

B] Identify the following intervals.

Unit Three Practice Test

A) Provide the key signature for the following major and minor keys.

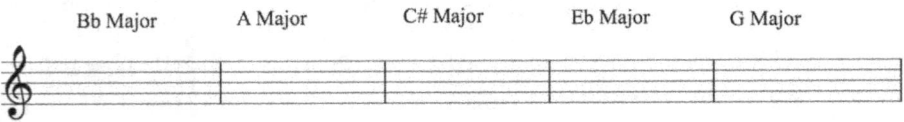

B) Provide the name of the major AND minor key for each key signature.

C) Provide the following notes ABOVE to complete the interval.

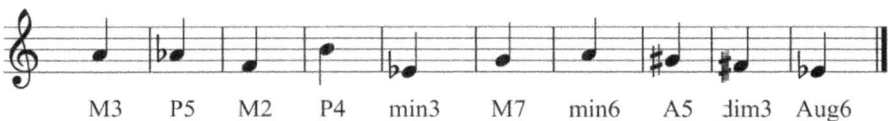

M3   P5   M2   P4   min3   M7   min6   A5   dim3   Aug6

Unit Four
Chords

Lesson 141

Harmony: Major Triads

Chords

A musical chord is any number of vertically stacked pitches. Here is a chord built on stacked perfect fourths.

Here is a chord based on fifths.

Here is a chord built on a variety of intervals.

Musical Triads

A triad is a particular type of chord built specifically on at least two thirds.

A major triad is a specific type of triad made up of a M3 (4 semitones) and P5 (+3 more semitones) from the bottom note.

The above triad is called the C major triad because C is the bottom note (tonic) and because it is built on the first, third, and fifth scale degrees of the C major scale.

To build a major triad, find the first, third, and fifth scale degrees on the note given. A quick way to learn to identify and create major triads is to memorize just seven and then alter them as needed. Notice the following seven major triads.

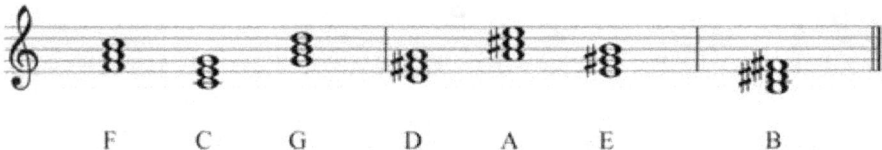

They are major triads whose tonic notes are based on the magic formula already encountered:

F C G D A E B

Notice that the first three triads contain no accidentals, the second three triads contain a sharp on the third of the chord, and the last triad contains a sharp on the third and fifth notes of the chord.

(1)F C G (2)D A E (3)B

Group 1 triads have no accidentals

<u>Group 2 triads have a sharp on the third of the chord</u>
<u>Group 3 has a sharp on the third and the fifth</u>

By remembering just these seven major triads you can figure out most other triads. For example, if asked to create a major triad on F# you could look at the F major triad and add sharps to all three notes to get the correct answer. By adding the same accidental to all the notes you are maintaining the same space in the triad.

F Major triad = F-A-C (Group 1 triad)

F# Major triad = F#-A#-C#

For another example try creating a major triad on Bb. Recall the B major triad and add a flat to each note of the triad. (Remember that flats cancel sharps and vice versa.)

B Major triad = B-D#-F# (Group 3 triad)

Bb Major triad = Bb-D-F

Triads in the Scale

If you write out the major scale and add triads to each note you get triad positions within that scale. For now, just notice the fact that different chords can appear in different positions in a scale. Each of these positions has a name which align directly with the name of the note in the scale. These are the names of the chords from the C Major scale.

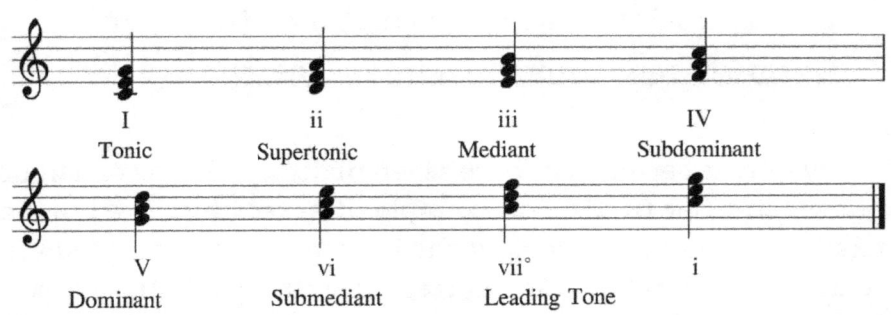

Exercise 141

Construct the following major triads:

1. F major

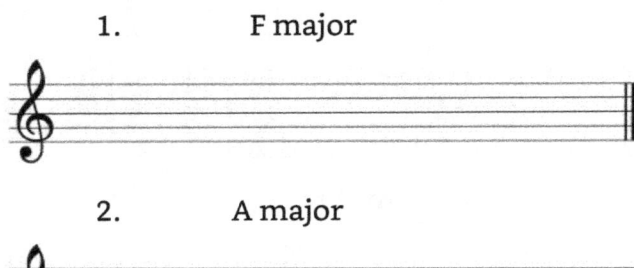

2. A major

3. Bb major

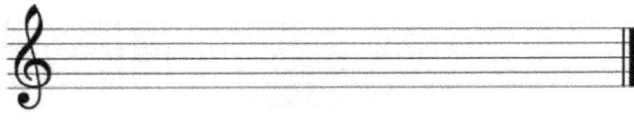

4. Eb major

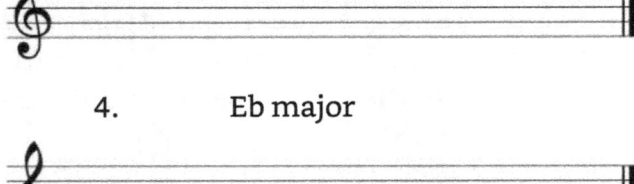

5. G# major

Steps for doing this exercise:
- Build the major scale from the note given.
- Pick out the 1st, 3rd, and 5th scale degrees to build the triad.

Homework 141

Build major chords on the following notes.

KENNETH P. LANGER

Lesson 142

Harmony: Minor and Altered Triads

The Minor Triad

Just like the major triad the minor triad can be found by taking the first, third and fifth scale degrees of the minor scale.

Another way of thinking of the minor triad is that it is similar to a major triad except that the third is lowered one semitone.

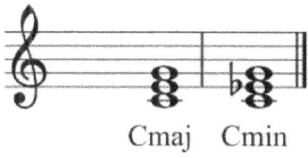

Cmaj   Cmin

Using the seven major triads (F C G D A E B) minor triads can be created by determining the major triad and lowering its third by a semitone. Compare the two types of triads in the chart below.

Triad	Third	Fifth
Major	M3	P5
Minor	min3	P5

Exercise 142a

Spell the following triads:

1] A minor

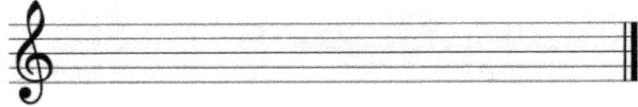

2] C minor

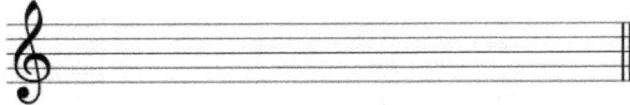

3] D minor

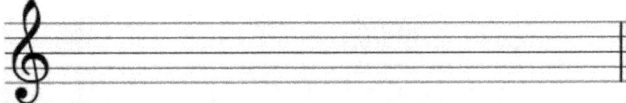

4] F# minor

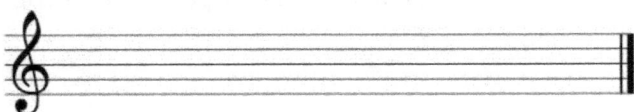

5] C# minor

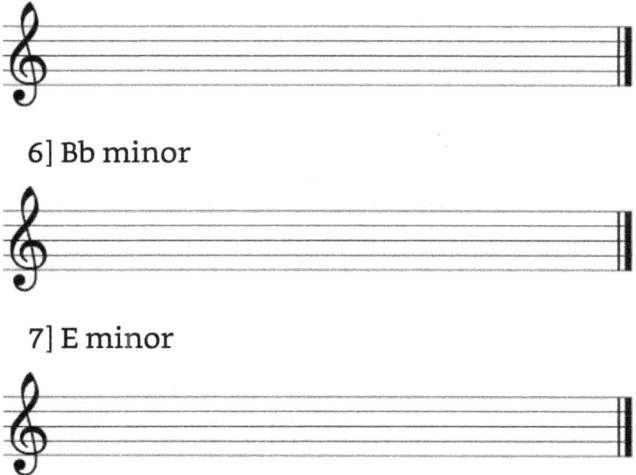

6] Bb minor

7] E minor

Steps for doing this exercise:
- Find the major triad using the seven letters method (or any method that works for you).
- Lower the third of the major triad down one half step.

Diminished and Augmented Triads

There are two other triads that are possible with stacked thirds. A diminished triad contains a minor third like the minor triad but also contains a lowered fifth (dim5). An augmented triad contains a major third and an augmented fifth.

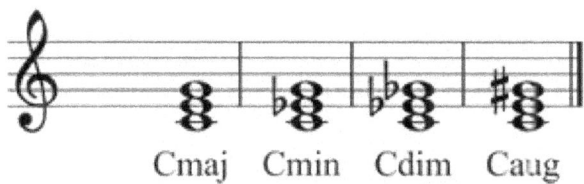

Compare all four kinds of triads in the following chart.

Triad	Third	Fifth
Major	M3	P5
Minor	min3	P5
Diminished	min3	dim5
Augmented	M3	Aug5

Each of the four triads is created by increasing or decreasing distances in the chord. If we compare differences between the triads in relation to the major triad we get the following chart.

Triad	Third	Fifth
Augmented		/\
Major		
Minor	\/	
Diminished	\/	\/

Minor, Diminished, and Augmented triads can be created by starting from the major triad and altering that triad.

C major triad: C - E - G
C minor triad: C - Eb - G
C augmented triad: C - E - G#
C diminished triad: C - Eb – Gb

Exercise 142b

Construct the following triads:

1. Gx Major

2. F minor

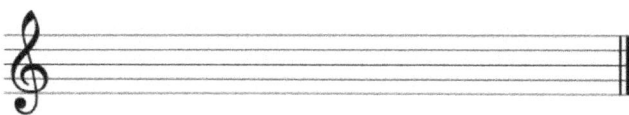

3. A minor

4. Eb minor

5. B diminished

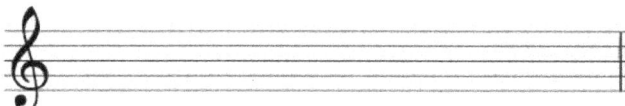

6. D diminished

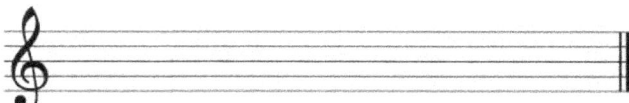

7. C# diminished

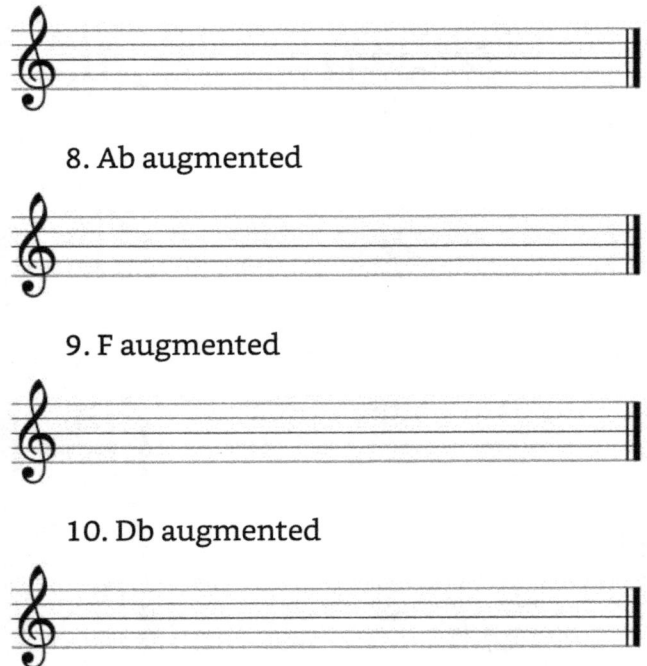

8. Ab augmented

9. F augmented

10. Db augmented

Homework 142

Construct the type of triad requested on the following notes.

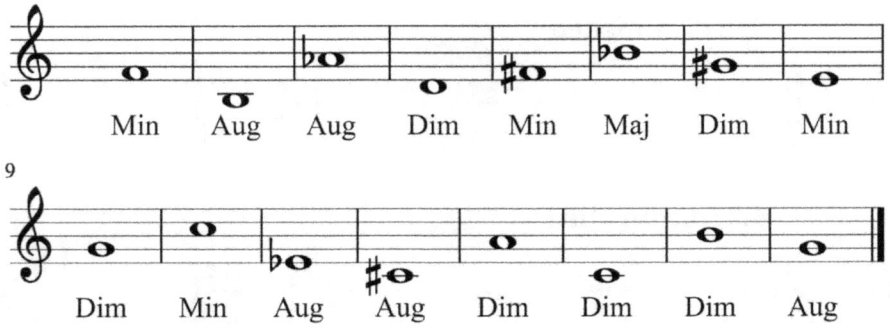

Lesson 143

Harmony: Chord Inversions

Triad Inversions

A triad can have inversions just like intervals. When an a triad is inverted its bottom note is moved up an octave. This can happen twice with every triad. Here is the C major triad with tonic on the bottom. This is known as root position.

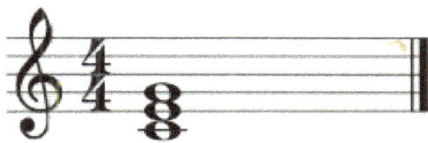

Here is a triad with the bottom note (tonic) moved up one octave. This is known as the first inversion of the triad.

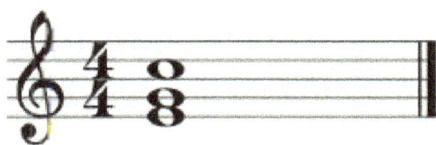

Here is a triad with the bottom note (tonic) and the middle note (the third) moved up one octave. This is known as the second inversion of the triad.

If the process was done again we would end up with the same

triad in the same position just one octave higher. Here is another way of looking at the inversions.

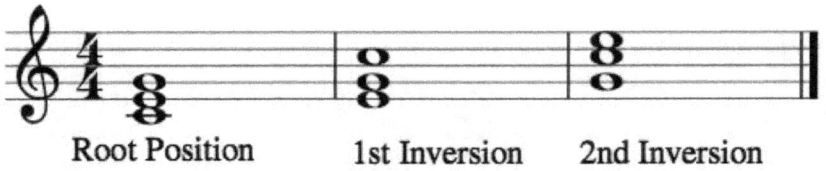

Root Position   1st Inversion   2nd Inversion

Open vs. Closed Position Triads

A triad that appears in its standard 1-3-5 formation like the first chord in the example above is said to be in closed position because there are no notes that can fit between them. Chords with notes in other octaves can be called open chords. Here is an open position C major triad.

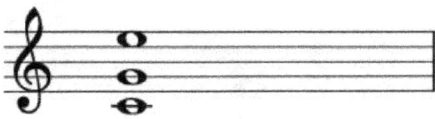

Regardless of whether or not a triad is open or closed, the only thing that determines the inversion is the lowest sounding note. See the chart below.

lowest sounding note	chord inversion
Tonic	root position
Third	1st inversion
Fifth	2nd inversion

Chords in Four Parts

Chords often appear in four parts because the standard vocal choir has four parts: soprano, alto, tenor, and bass. Since a triad has only three notes and a choir has four parts, one of the notes of the triad has to be doubled. Here is an example of four part chordal writing with doubled notes. Notice the chord names above and the position of the chords within the scale below. (From the hymn tune * "Toulon.")

Exercise 143

(1) Construct the following triads in their position:

(a) D major - root position

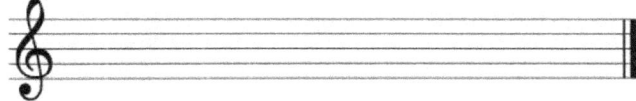

(b) G minor - 1st inversion

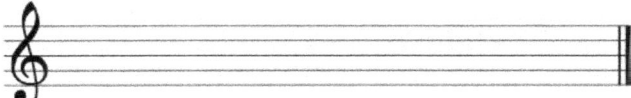

(c) C diminished - 2nd inversion

(d) Eb major - root position

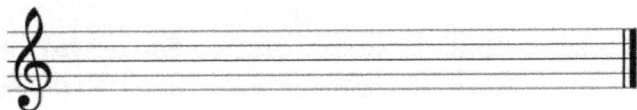

(e) A# minor - 1st inversion

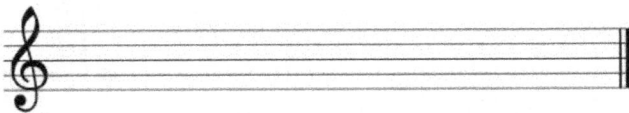

(f) Bb augmented - 2nd inversion

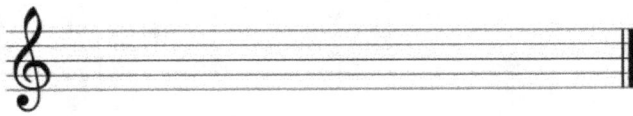

(2) Figure out the following four part chords and their inversions.

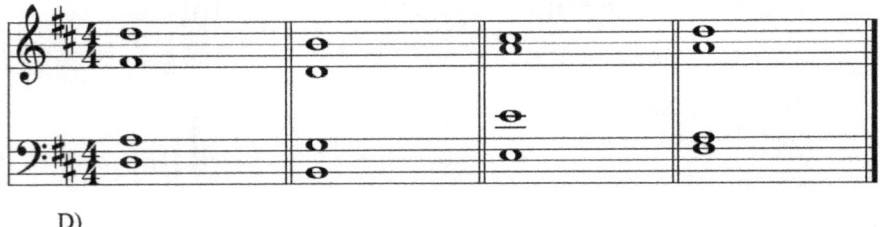

D)

Homework 143

Construct triads with the requested inversions.

A THEORY FOR ALL MUSIC

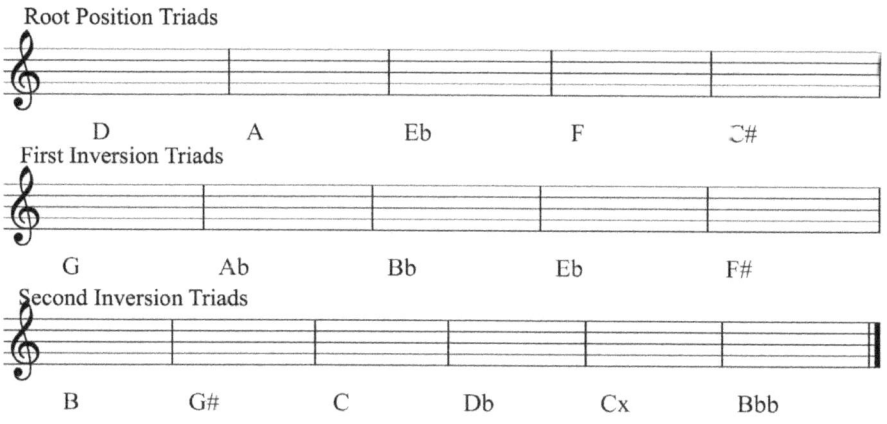

Unit Four Practice Test

Provide notes to complete the following triads.

C Maj - root position   B Maj - 1st inversion   Ab Maj - 2nd inversion

F min - root position   Ab min - 1st inversion   D# min - 2nd inversion

Db aug - root position   G aug - 1st inversion   F# aug - 2nd inversion

C# dim - root position   A dim - 1st inversion   Bb dim - 2nd inversion

Unit Five

Harmonic Analysis

Lesson 151

Harmony: Macro Analysis

Definition

Macro-analysis is a method of identifying chords in a piece of music.

With macro-analysis three things are defined:

(1) The root of the chord

(2) The quality of the chord

    (a) major (M)

    (b) minor (min)

    (c) augmented (+)

    (d) diminished (o)

(3) The lowest sounding note of the chord

The root of the chord is indicated by the note name, the quality by three letter designations (except major), and the lowest sounding note with a slash and a letter name. The chart below shows the symbols used for chords based on C.

Chord	Symbol
C major	C or CΔ

C minor	C min or c-
C diminished	c°
C augmented	C+
C major - 1st inversion	C/E
C major - 2nd inversion	C/G

Typically, the macro analysis symbols are placed above the score in the same way that contemporary music adds chord symbols above the top line.

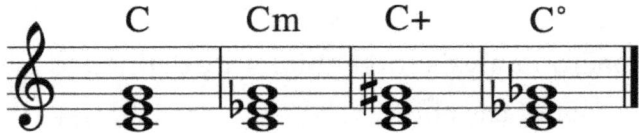

Note: In your assignments, please distinguish major from minor by using capital letters for major chords (C = C Major) and the letters "min" for minor (Cmin = C minor).

Chord Relationships

In addition to this information, solid curved lines are used to show dominant to tonic relationships and dotted curved lines are used to show leading-tone to tonic relationships.

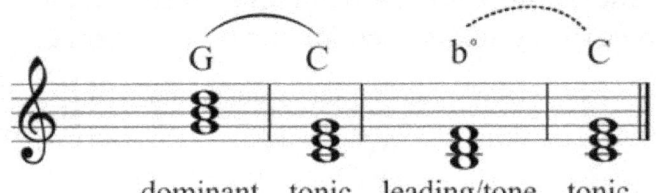

Here is an example of a macro analysis of a section of a chorale. The work is ? J.S. Bach: "Ach Gott Und Herr." It has been altered for this demonstration.

A THEORY FOR ALL MUSIC

Application

Below is an analysis of * *Beethoven's "Moonlight Sonata"* showing macro or contemporary analysis above the score. Connecting curves have not been added in this analysis.

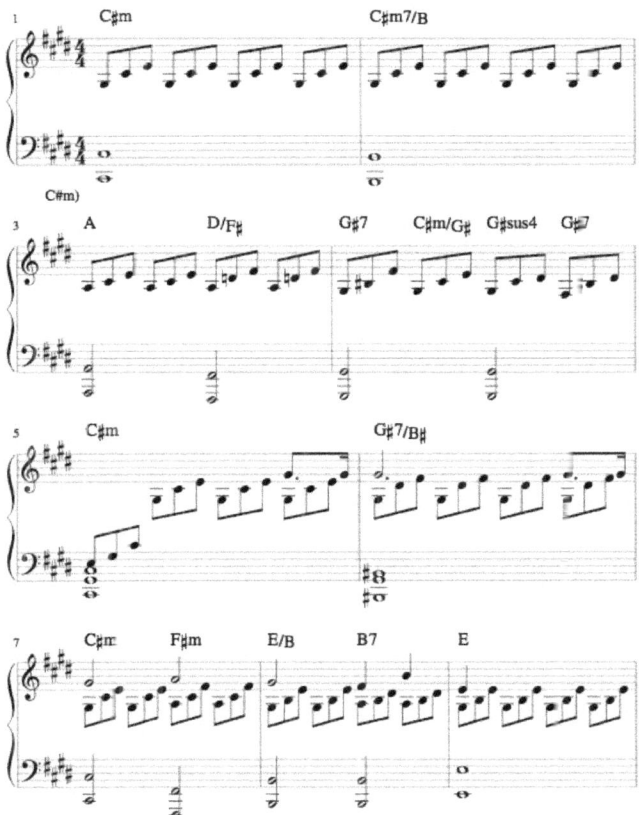

Exercise 151

Place macro-analysis symbols above the chords of the following Bach Chorale:

Homework 151

Provide a macro analysis.

A THEORY FOR ALL MUSIC

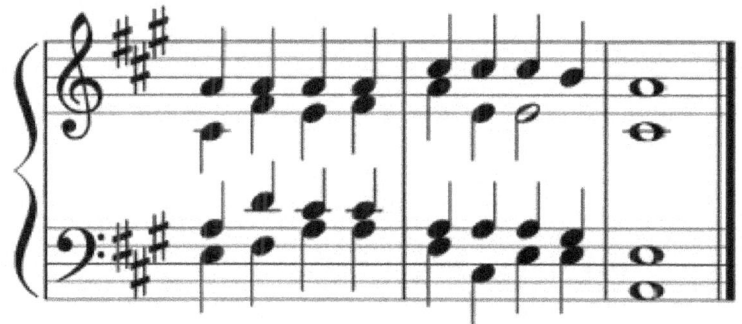

Lesson 152

Harmony: Roman Numeral Analysis

Definition

Roman Numeral analysis is the classical method of chord analysis. It provides the same information as macro-analysis but with one added piece of information: chord position within a key. This method of analysis uses roman numerals to indicate where each chord is within the scale of the key. The quality of a chord is indicated by the type of roman numeral, the roman numeral number indicates the chord position in the key, and additional arabic numerals are used to indicate inversions.

- Type of roman numeral = quality of the chord
- Number = chord position
- Arabic numbers = inversions

Triads in the Scale

If triads are created on each degree of a scale we can number those triads by position.

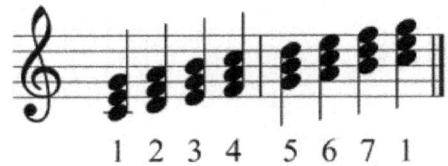

Notice also that each chord has a different quality. It is a good idea to remember the qualities of chords in major and minor keys. Here are the qualities of the chords in the major scale.

Here are the roman numerals of the chords of the major scale.

Roman Numeral analysis indicates both chord position and quality. The chord position is done by number and quality by capital and small case letters.

Chord quality	Roman Numeral	Sample on Tonic Chord
Major	capital letter	I
minor	small letter	i
diminished	small letter with circle	i°
Augmented	capital letter with plus	I+

Observe the use of roman numerals to indicate the position and quality of each chord in the major scale.

Here are the chords based on the harmonic minor scale.

Notice the three altered chords (III+, V, and vii°).

Inversions

Inversions with Roman Numeral Analysis are done by adding Arabic numbers that indicate the distance from the bottom note to the notes above it. It was learned that a major triad is created by adding a M3 and a P5 above the tonic note. We could call that chord a I5/3 but the 5 and the 3 are usually understood and left out so the root position tonic chord is just called a I chord.

A first inversion chord has a 6th and a 3rd above it. Again the 3 is left out leaving the 6 so a first inversion tonic chord is called a I6.

A second inversion chord has a 6th and a 4th above it so a tonic second inversion chord would be called a I6/4.

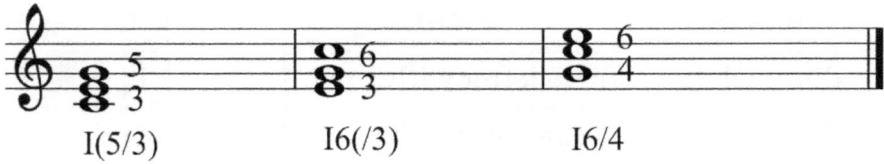

Application

Here is the same * *Beethoven: Moonlight Sonata* from the last unit. Observe the Roman Numeral Analysis below. (Note: not all symbols will be familiar.)

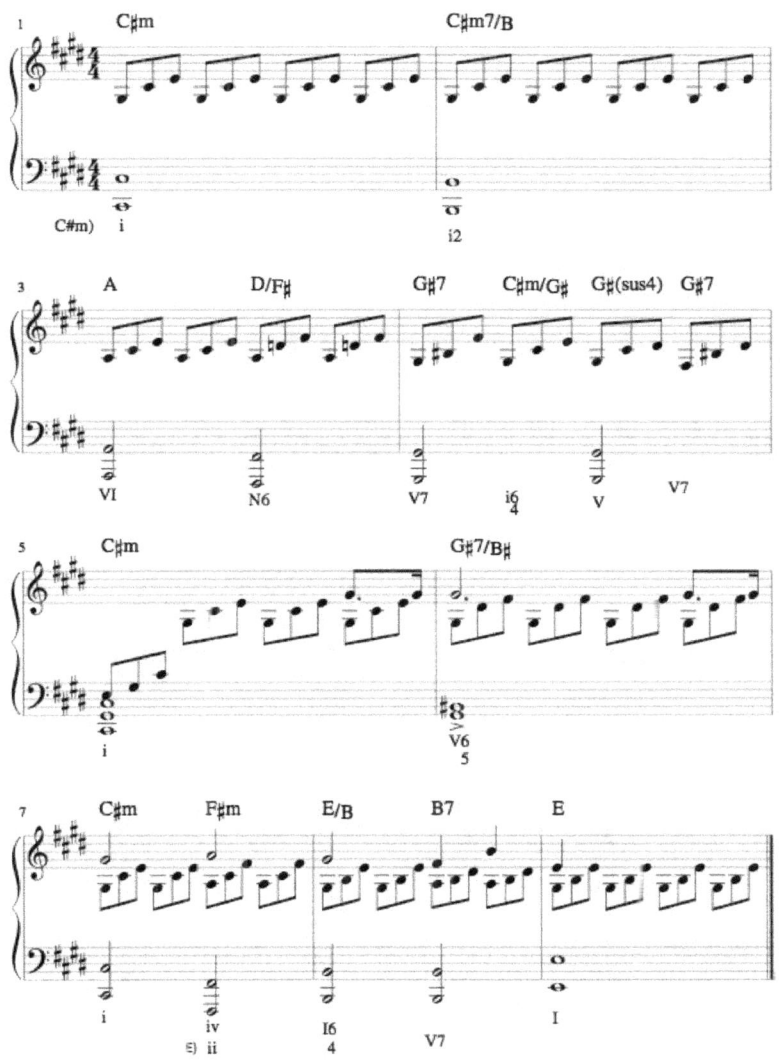

Exercise 152

Do a Roman Numeral Analysis of the following work. Place the symbols underneath.

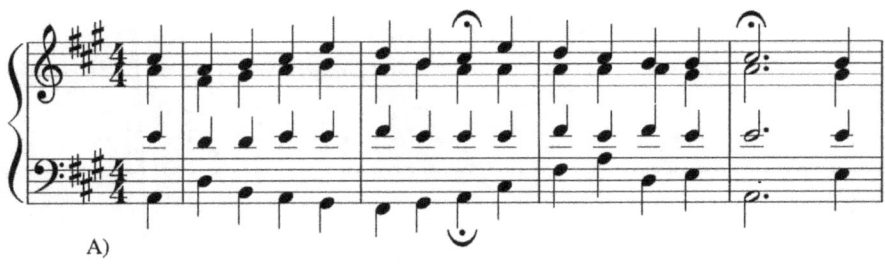

A)

Homework 152

Provide a roman numeral analysis underneath.

A)

Lesson 153
Harmony: Cadences

Definition

A cadence is a musical device used to separate musical ideas. You can think of a cadence like the punctuation that ends or breaks a sentence. A musical sentence (called a phrase) is often ended by some type of cadence.

Types of Cadences

Cadences can be created through:
- Melody
- Rhythm
- Harmony

Melodic Cadence

Melodic cadences happen (usually in conjunction with rhythmic and/or harmonic cadences) when the melody moves towards tonic–often in a downward motion. In this two phrase example in A minor, the two phrases are marked by curved lines (called phrase markings). Notice how the melody moves generally down to G# in the first phrase, rises again, then goes down to the tonic A at the end of the second phrase. (* *Leopold Mozart: Entree*)

Rhythmic Cadence

A rhythmic cadence happens when the rhythmic motion of a phrase is interrupted or stopped. This can be done with a note with a longer duration than the other notes in the phrase or by adding rests. In the above example, the only whole note that appears is at the end of the second phrase. This whole note greatly slows down the rhythmic motion of the melody. It functions as a rhythmic cadence.

Harmonic Cadence

A harmonic cadence is a specific pattern of chords used at the end of a phrase. These patterns have become recognized as standard chord movements that help to define phrase endings.

There are four of these standard patterns:

(1) the Authentic Cadence

    (a) perfect authentic

    (b) imperfect authentic

(2) the Plagal Cadence
(3) the Half Cadence
(4) the Deceptive Cadence

The Authentic Cadence

The Authentic Cadence has a chord pattern of V-I or V-i. There are two types of Authentic Cadences:
(1) The Perfect Authentic Cadence
(2) The Imperfect Authentic Cadence.

The Perfect Authentic Cadence (PAC)

In order for a cadence to be called a Perfect Authentic Cadence, it must contain the following:
(1) The final two chords of the phrase must be V-I or V-i.
(2) The V chord must be major.
(3) Both chords must be in root position.
(4) The last highest note must be tonic.

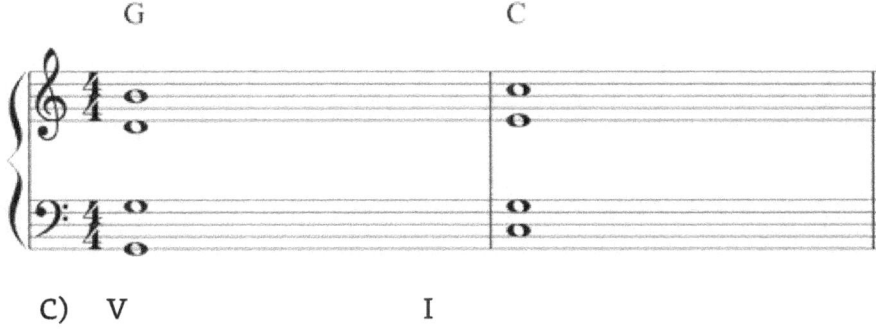

The PAC is the strongest cadence and marks a clear and complete ending to a phrase.

The Imperfect Authentic Cadence (IAC)

A dominant to tonic cadence that does not meet ALL of these conditions is named an Imperfect Authentic Cadence.

Sometimes a vii° chord can substitute for the V to create a vii°-I IAC.

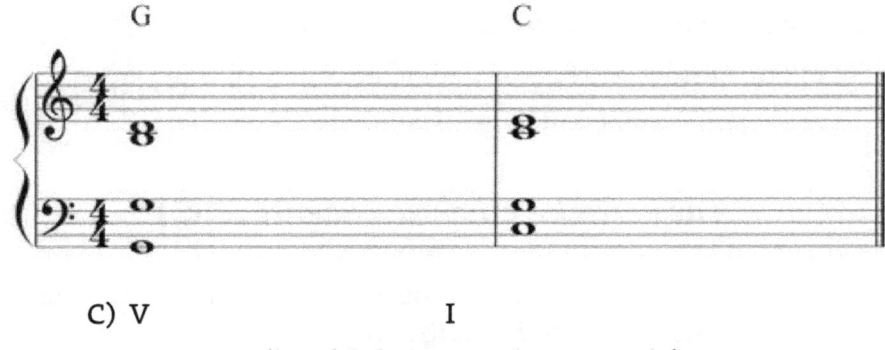

C) V   I

(last highest note is not tonic)

The Plagal Cadence (PC)

The Plagal Cadence employs the chords IV-I or iv-i.

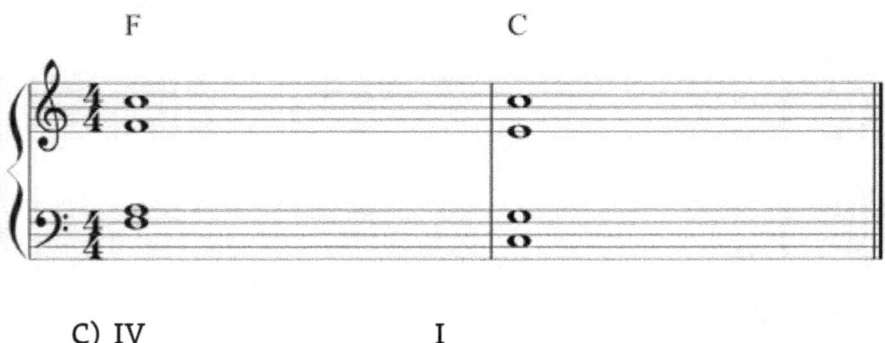

C) IV   I

The Half Cadence (HC)

A Half Cadence ends on V.

A THEORY FOR ALL MUSIC

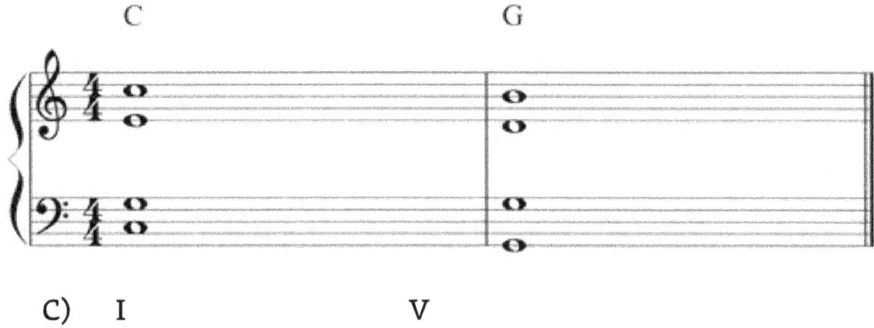

There is a special half cadence called the Phrygian Half Cadence that uses the chords IV6-V.

The Deceptive Cadence (DC)

A Deceptive Cadence ends on vi (or VI). It is sometimes called an Interrupted Cadence.

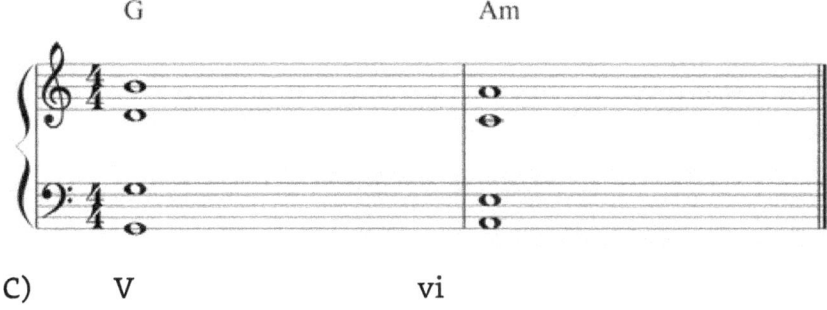

Exercise 153

Identify the cadence at the end of each four measure phrase.

Homework 153

- Analyze the chords.
- Identify the cadence.

A THEORY FOR ALL MUSIC

Lesson 154

Harmony: Non-Chord Tones

Definition

A non-chord tone is a note that appears but which is not part of the intended triad.

Non-Chord Tones

Non-chord tones can be accented or unaccented. They are accented if they appear on the same beat as the chord. They are unaccented if they appear between chords. Non-chord tones are defined by the notes that come before and after.

The Most Common Non-Chord Tones

The three types of non-chord tones that are most often encountered are the passing tone, the neighbor tone, and the suspension.

The Passing Tone (PT)

The most common of all non-chord tones is the passing tone. The passing tone is approached and resolved stepwise in the same direction so that the overall motion is scale-wise. Here is an unaccented passing tone (the note in red). Observe the notes before and after it.

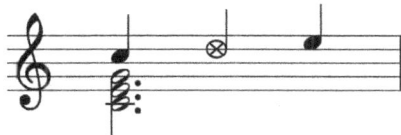

Here is an accented passing tone.

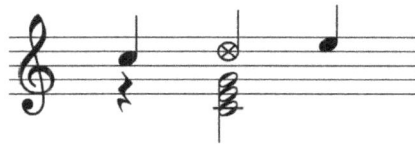

The Neighboring Tone (NT)

Another very common non-chord tone is the neighboring tone. It is also approached and resolved by a step but the two surrounding notes are the same.

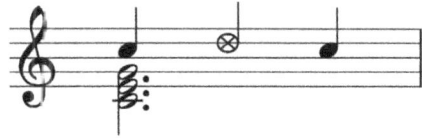

The Suspended Tone (Sus) and Retardation (Ret)

The suspended tone is a note that is consonant in one chord but becomes dissonant when maintained into another chord and is then resolved downwards. The suspended tone can sometimes be identified with "sus" in macro analysis and popular music symbols.

A retardation is similar to a suspension except that it resolves upwards.

Other Non-Chord Tones

The Anticipation (Ant)

The Appoggiatura (App)

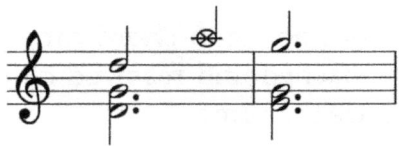

The Escape Tone (ET)

The Pedal Tone (Ped)

In this example, the pedal tone is the sustained note in the bass.

Table of Non-Chord Tones

The following table compares together all the non-chord tones (NCT) presented here by observing the two notes that surround each. The note before is called the Approach and the note after is called the Resolution.

NCT	Approach	Resolution	Outer Interval
PT	step	step	third
NT	step	step	unison
Sus	unison	step down	second
Ret	unison	step up	second
Ant	step	unison	second
App	leap	step	varies
ET	step	leap	varies
Ped	unison	unison	N/A

Exercise 154

- Analyze the chords.
- Identify the cadences.
- Mark and identify all the non-chord tones in the following example.

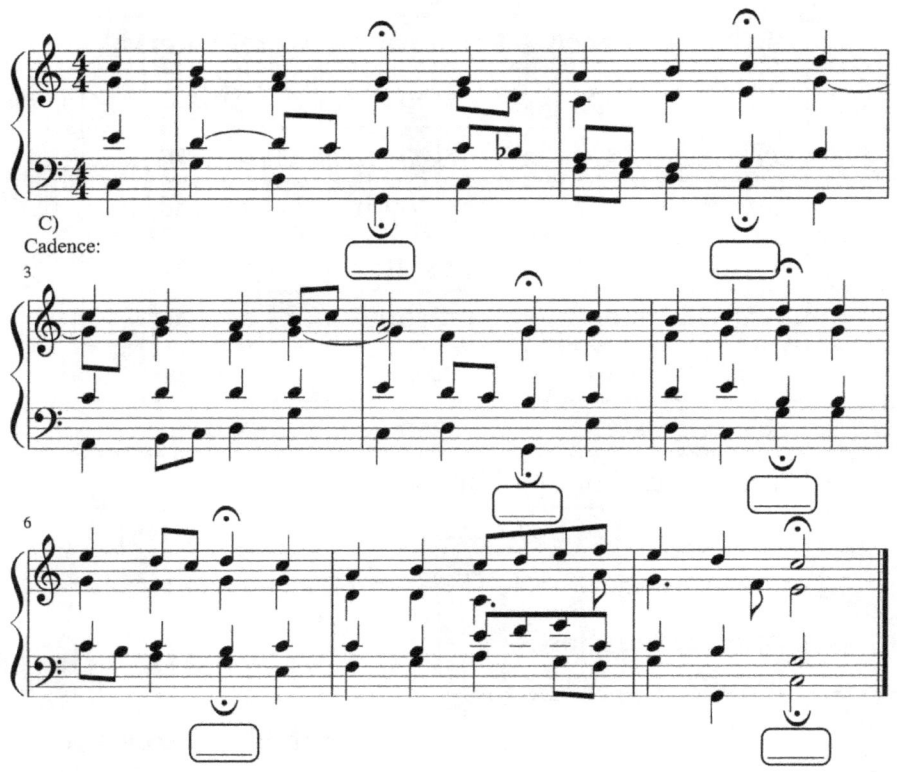

Homework 154

- Analyze the chords.
- Identify the cadences.
- Mark and identify all the non-chord tones in the following example.

D)

Lesson 155
Complete Analysis

Putting It All Together

In this lesson we will put together all that has been discussed in Book One. Practice by analyzing the provided piece for the following:

(1) the key

(2) a macro-analysis above

(3) a roman numeral analysis below

(4) find and identify cadences

    (a) In these exercises, cadences will be at the fermatas.

(5) identify all non-harmonic tones

Sample Analysis

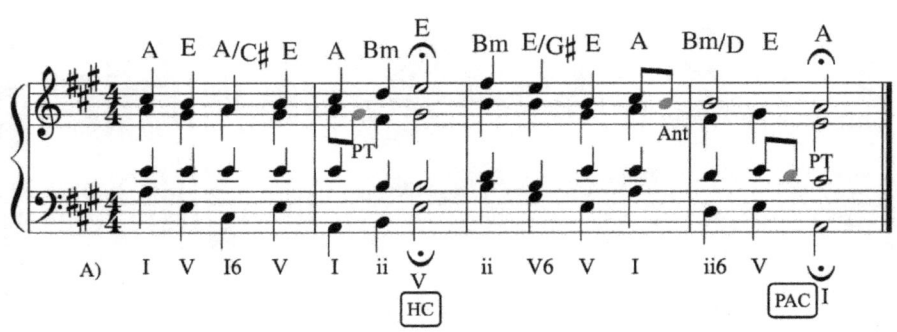

Exercise 155

Analyze the following piece of music for:
(1) The key
(2) The macro-analysis
(3) The roman numeral analysis
(4) The cadences
(5) The non-harmonic tones.

Additional Practice

1)

C)

2)

A)

3)

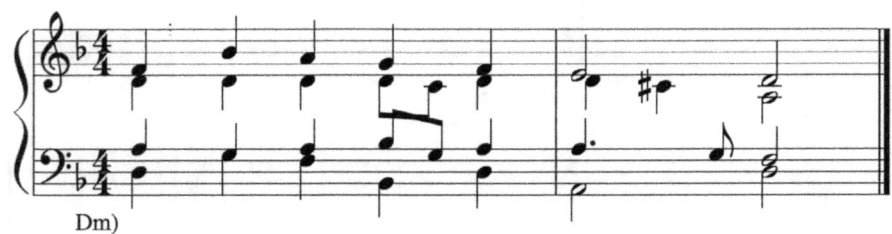

Dm)

Unit Five Practice Test

Provide the following:
1. A macro analysis above.
2. A roman numeral analysis below.
3. Identify the type of cadence at each fermata.

Exercise Answers

Unit One Answers

Exercise 111 Answers

Answer the following sentences with note or rest duration symbols.

1. Two quarter notes = 1 half

2. Two half notes = 1 W

3. Two eighth notes = 1 q

4. Two sixteenth notes = 1 e

5. Four quarter notes = 1 W

6. Two quarter rests = 1 _•_ (half rest)

7. Two half rests = 1 • (whole rest)

8. Two eighth rests = 1 Œ

9. Two sixteenth rests = 1 ‰

Exercise 112 Answers

If the quarter note is the pulse unit, how many beats would each of the following notes receive?

1) whole note = 4
2) half note = 2

If the dotted quarter note is the pulse unit, how many beats would each of the following notes receive?

3) dotted whole note = 4

4) dotted half note = 2

If the half note is the pulse unit, how many beats would each of the following notes receive?

5) whole note = 2

6) half note = 1

Exercise 113 Answers

Identify a most likely pulse unit for each example. See if you can feel the pulse beat and tap or clap along with it.

A) Schindler's List Theme: The quarter note

B) Pink: The quarter note

C) Vivaldi: The dotted quarter note

D) Slow Dance: The half note

Exercise 114 Answers

1)

2)

A THEORY FOR ALL MUSIC

Exercise 115 Answers

A) 5/4

B) 9/8

C) 7/8

D) 2/4

Unit One Practice Test Answers

A] Provide rest or duration symbols for each. For example: 2 eighth notes = 1: quarter note

    Two quarter rests = 1 half rest

    Two half rests = 1 whole rest

    Two eighth notes = 1 quarter note

    Two quarter notes = 1 half note

    Two half notes = 1 whole note

    Eight sixteenth notes = 2 quarter notes

    Four quarter notes = 2 half notes

    Four quarter rests = 2 half rests

B] Identify the duration of each note:

    If the pulse is a quarter note, what is the duration of a:

    dotted half note = 3 beats

    whole note = 4 beats

    If the pulse is a dotted quarter note, what is the duration of a:

    dotted half note = 2 beats

    dotted whole note = 4 beats

C] What is the pulse unit for the following time signatures:

    4/4 = quarter note

    6/8 = eighth note

    5/2 = half note

D] Beam according to the given pulse unit.
Pulse unit = quarter note

A THEORY FOR ALL MUSIC

Pulse unit = dotted quarter note

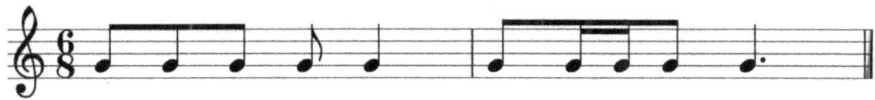

V. Determine the meter signature for each

Unit Two Answers

Exercise 121 Answers

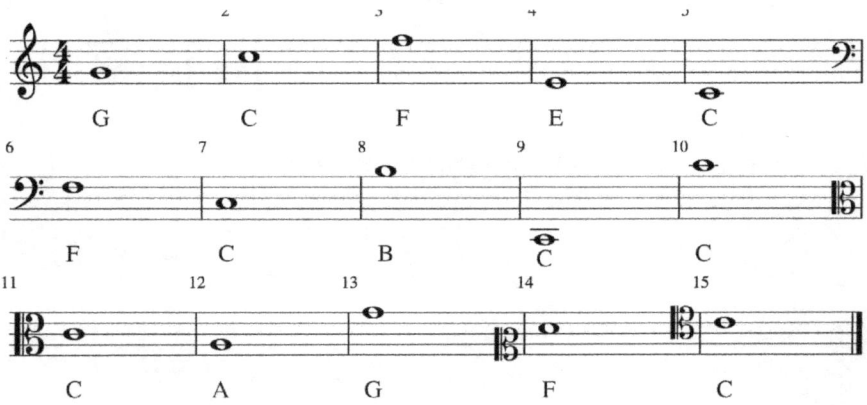

Exercise 122 Answers

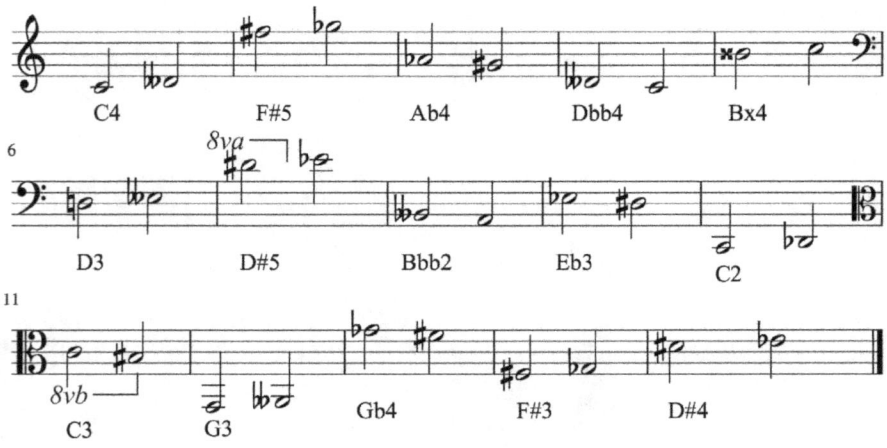

Exercise 123 Answers

1. Forte (dynamic marking) f = play the music loud
2. Mezzopiano (dynamic marking) P = play the music moderately soft
3. Crescendo (dynamic marking) < = get gradually louder
4. Sforzando (articulation) sfz = strong attack and release of a note
5. Staccato (articulation) . = play the note short and with space
6. Andante (tempo) = play the music at a walking pace
7. Ritardando (tempo) = gradually slow down the music

- Allegro (tempo) means play the music at a fast tempo at about 144 quarter notes per minute.
- Legato (articulation) means to play the notes full length with little space. (Sempre means somewhat.)
- Piano (dynamic) means play the music softly.
- Crescendo (dynamic) means gradually get louder.
- The dot by the notes is a Staccato (articulation) which

means play the notes short.

Exercise 124 Answers

1) G

2) B

3) Eb

4) Bb

Exercise 125 Answers

A THEORY FOR ALL MUSIC

Unit 2 Practice Test Answers

A] Identify each note by octave number.

1) D5   2) A4   3) Eb4   4) C#5   5) F5   6) F#3   7) C#3   8) C4
9) G2   10) Eb3   11) C4   12) G#4   13) Ab3   14) D4   15) A3

B] Write the following scales.

Unit Three Answers

Exercise 131 Answers

A] Construct the following key signatures in treble and bass clefs.

D major

F# major

Ab major

Bb major

B] Identify the following key signatures.

a)
B Major

b)
Gb Major

Exercise 132 Answers

1) Construct the following key signatures:

a) Bb minor

b) G# minor

c) F minor

d) F# minor

2) Identify the following minor key signatures.

E minor

Eb minor

Exercise 133 Answers

1) Write the note that completes the following intervals:
    a) M2 above F# = G#
    b) P5 above Ab = Eb

c) M3 above F = A
d) M6 above Bb = G
e) P4 above D = A
f) M7 above E = D#

2) Identify the following intervals:
a)

P5

b)

M3

c)

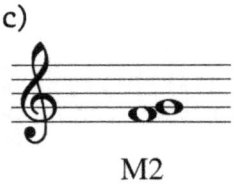

M2

Exercise 134 Answers

1) Provide the note for the following intervals above:
   a) M3 above Ab = C
   b) M7 above E = D#
   c) M2 above Bbb = Cb
   d) M6 above Ab = F
   e) P5 above F# = C#
   f) P4 above Bb = Eb

g) A4 above C = F#
h) d5 above Dx = A#
i) min3 above D = F
j) min6 above G# = E

2) Provide the note for the following intervals below:
   a) M2 below C = Bb
   b) M7 below C# = D
   c) P5 below Eb = Ab
   d) M3 below G# = E
   e) A5 below F# = Bb

3) Identify the following intervals:
   P8   min7   min6   A4   dim4   M2   PU

Unit 3 Practice Test Answers

A) Provide the key signature for the following major and minor keys.

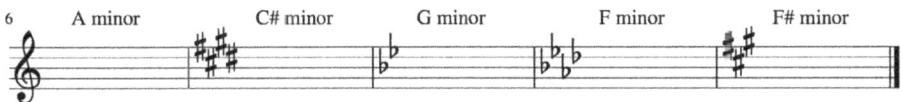

B) Provide the name of the major AND minor key for each key signature.

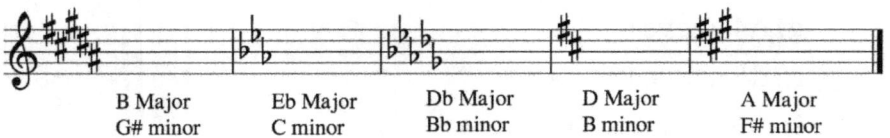

| B Major | Eb Major | Db Major | D Major | A Major |
| G# minor | C minor | Bb minor | B minor | F# minor |

C) Provide the following notes to complete the interval.

M3   P5   M2   P4   min3   M7   min6   A5   dim3   Aug6

Unit Four Answers

Exercise 141 Answers

Construct the following major triads:

1. F major = F-A-C
2. A major = A-C#-E
3. Bb major = Bb-D-F
4. Eb major = Eb-G-Bb
5. G# major = G#-B#-D#
6. Db major = Db-F-Ab
7. F# major = F#, A#, C#
8. Abb major = Abb, Cb, Ebb
9. D# major = D#, Fx, A#

Exercise 142 Answers

Exercise 142a

Spell the following triads:

1. A minor = A-C-E
2. C minor = C-Eb-G
3. D minor = D-F-A
4. F# minor = F#-A-C#
5. C# minor = C#-E-G#
6. Bb minor = Bb-Db-F

7. E minor = E-G-B

Exercise 142b

Construct the following triads:
    a) Gx Major = Gx-Bx-Dx
    b) F minor = F-Ab-C
    c) A minor = A-C-E
    d) Eb minor = Eb-Gb-Bb
    e) B diminished = B-D-F
    f) D diminished = D-F-Ab
    g) C# diminished = C#-E-G
    h) Ab augmented = Ab-C-E
    i) F augmented = F-A-C#
    j) Db augmented = Db-F-A

Exercise 143 Answers

A] Construct the following triads in their position:
    a) D major - root position = D-F#-A
    b) G minor - 1st inversion = Bb-D-G
    c) C diminished - 2nd inversion = Gb-C-Eb
    d) Eb major - root position = Eb-G-Bb
    e) A# minor - 1st inversion = C#-E#-A#
    f) Bb augmented - 2nd inversion = F#-Bb-D

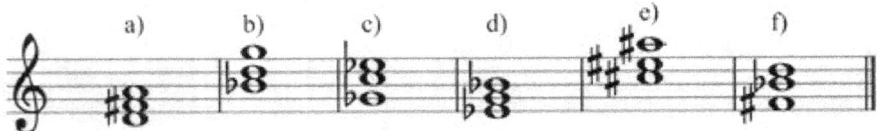

B]

A THEORY FOR ALL MUSIC

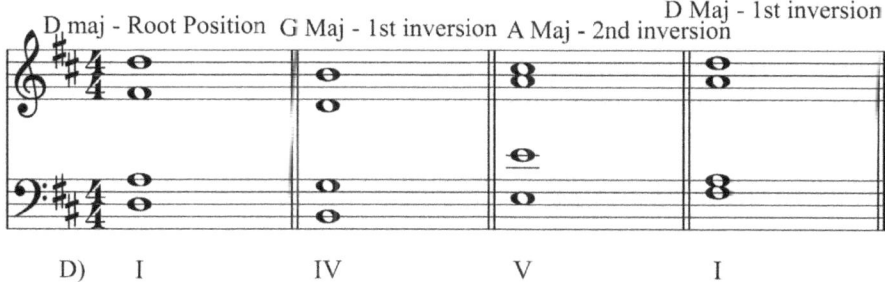

Unit Four Practice Test Answers

Provide notes to complete the following triads.

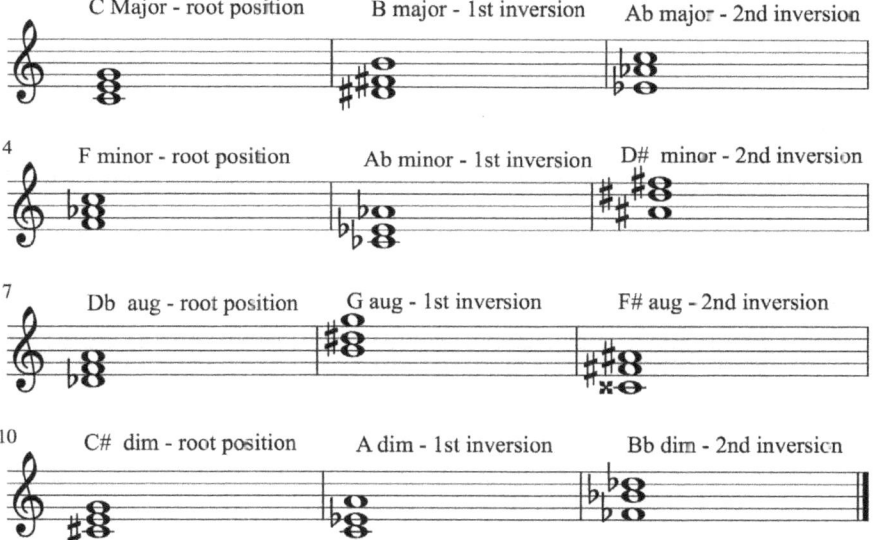

Unit Five Answers

Exercise 151 Answers

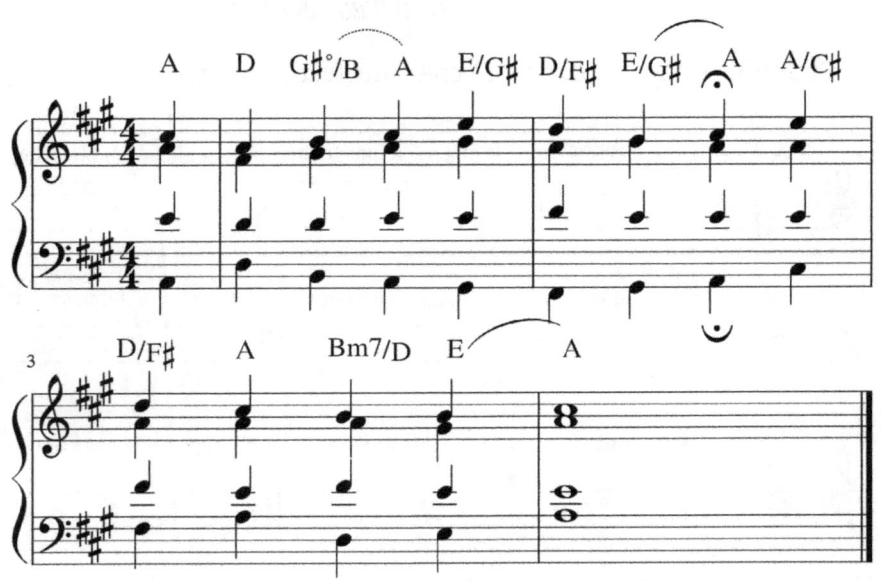

Exercise 152 Answers

A THEORY FOR ALL MUSIC

Exercise 153 Answers

Identify the cadence at the end of each four measure phrase.

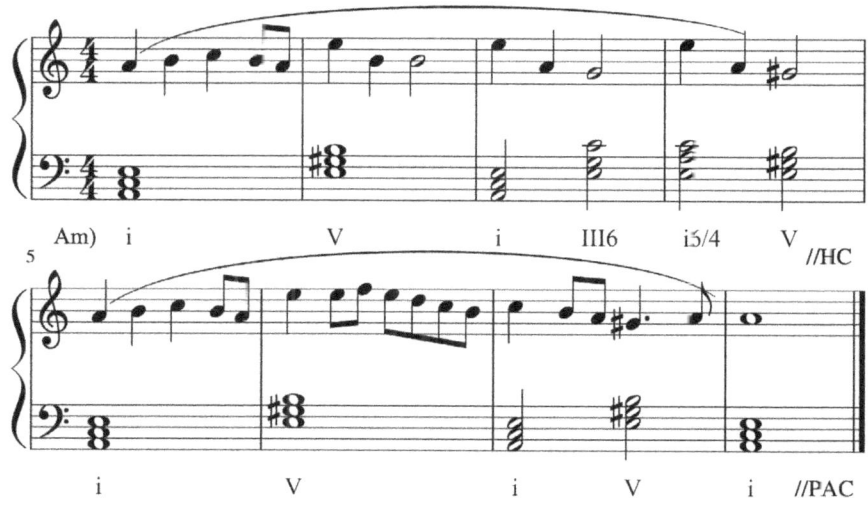

Exercise 154 Answers

(PT (7th) means a note that could be analyzed as the 7th of a chord rather than a NHT.)

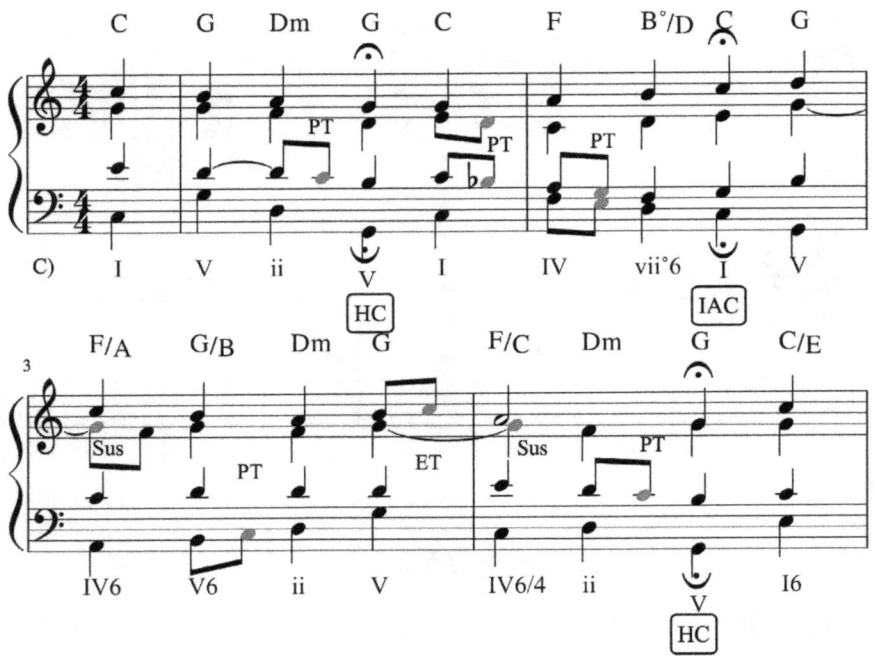

A THEORY FOR ALL MUSIC

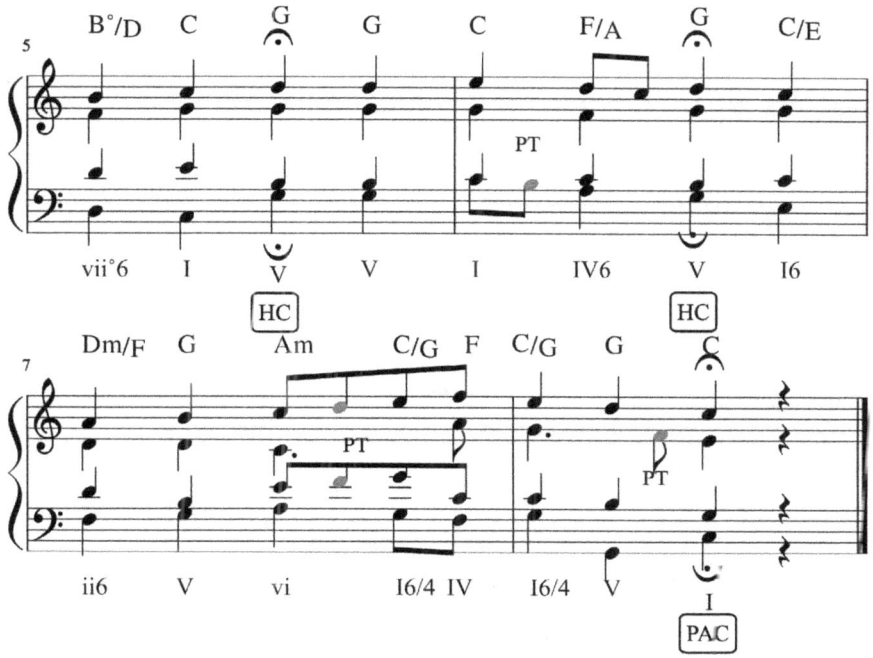

Exercise 155 Answers

A THEORY FOR ALL MUSIC

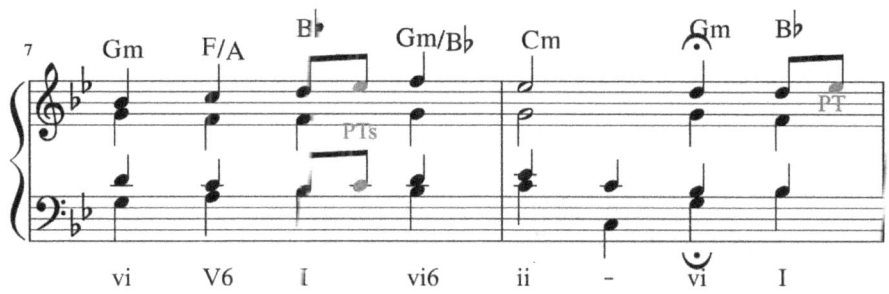

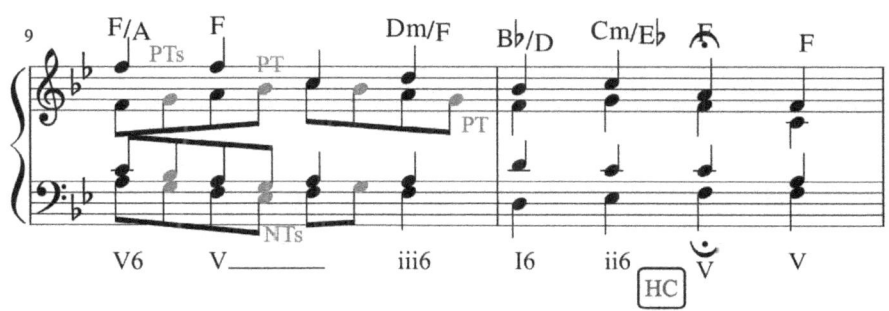

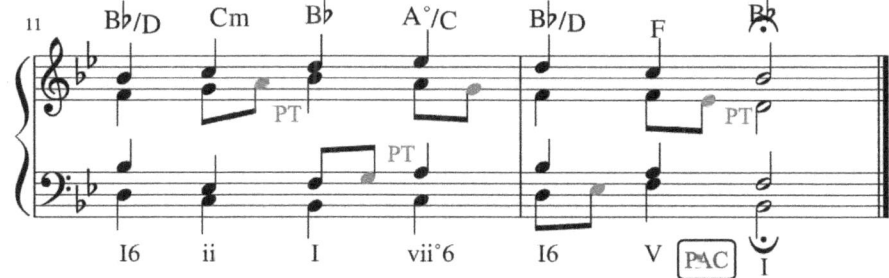

Practice 1 Answers

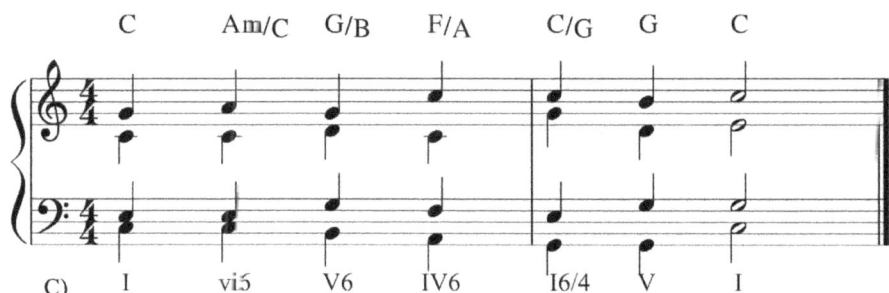

Practice 2 Answers

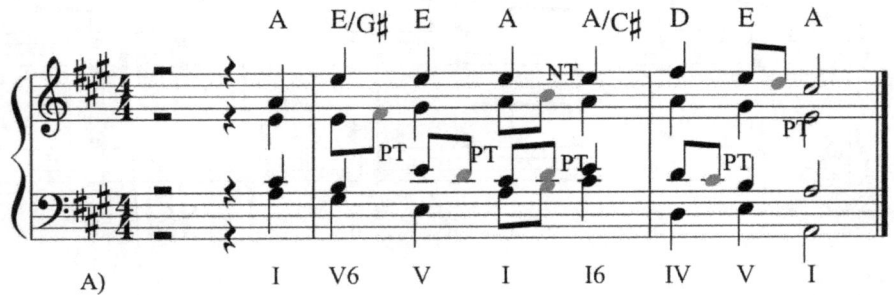

Practice 3 Answers

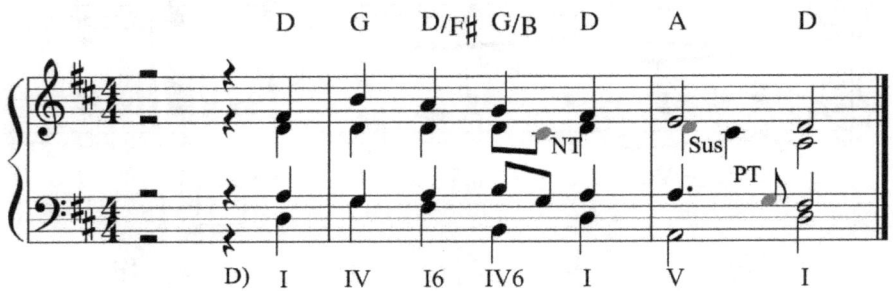

Unit Five Practice Test Answers

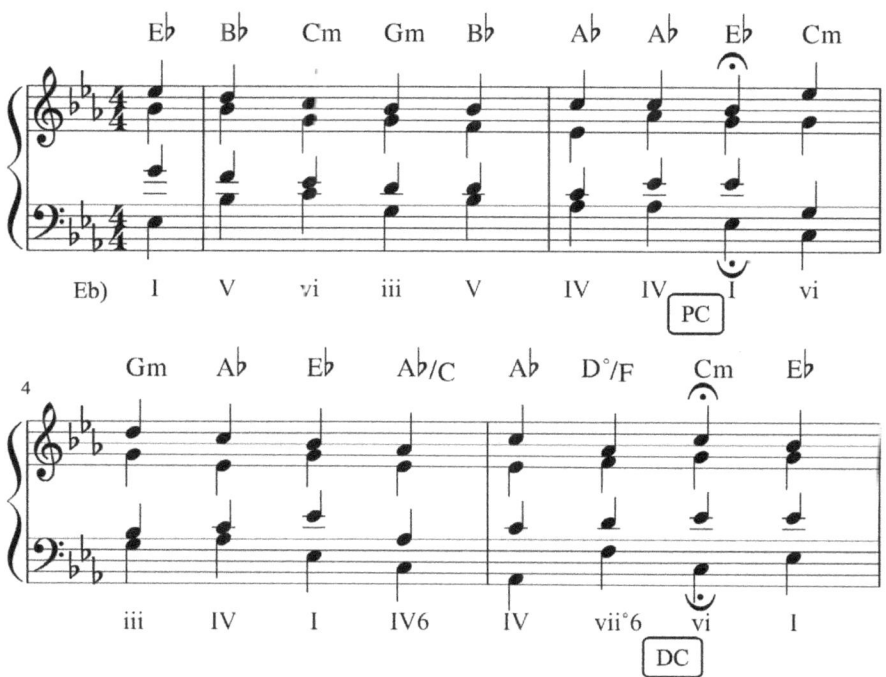

Other Books

Non-Fiction

- Spirituality
  - A Different Calling: A Manual for Lay Ministers and Other Non-Professional Facilitators of Any Spiritual Tradition
  - Many Leaves, One Tree: A Collection of Aphorisms Inspired by the Tao Te Ching
  - The Purpose Derived Life: What In The Universe Am I Here For?
  - Three Guidelines for Ethical Living
  - Playing Cards and the Game of Living Well
  - The Emergence of God: The Intersection of Science, Nature, and Spirituality
  - The Langer Deck
  - Emergent Spirituality: Principles and Practices at the Intersection of Science, Nature, and Spirituality
  - Open Hearts and Open Doors: Radical Hospitality in the Church
  - Let Us Wander: A Ministry of Music and Arts
- Games
  - 52 New Card Games (For Those Old Cards)
  - 36 New Dice Games
  - 40 Games for Forty Dice
  - Castle Imbroglio: An Escape Adventure Book
- Music
  - A Guide to the Art of Musical Performance

- A Theory for All Music
  - Book 1: Fundamentals
  - Book 2: Chords and Part-Writing
  - Book 3: The Tools of Analysis
  - Book 4: Parametric Analysis
- Rounds and Canons for Peace and Justice
- Music for Unitarian-Universalist Choirs
- Songs of Worship
- 50 Songs for Meditation

Fiction

- Science Fiction
  - The Milleran Cluster Series
    - Of Eternal Light
    - The Forever Horizon
    - The Suicide Fire
    - The Song of the Mother
    - The Journey of Awri
- Theater
  - Four Comedies
  - 10 x 10: Ten Ten-Minute Plays Book 1
  - 10 x 10: Ten Ten-Minute Plays Book 2
  - 10 x 10: Ten Ten-Minute Plays Book 3
  - 10 x 10: Ten Ten-Minute Plays Book 4
  - Ageless Wisdom: Multigenerational Plays for Worship
- Poetry
  - Looking At The World: A Collection of Poetry
  - Prayers

Final Note

Thank you for reading this book!

If you enjoyed reading it please let me know
and please consider writing a positive online review.

Ken Langer

<u>Contact Information</u>
personal website: http://kennethplanger.com
book site: http://brassbellbooks.com
Email: revklanger@gmail.com